I0159791

Thoughts and Prayers

Dr. Cedrick D. Bridgeforth

Copyright © 2012
323 Publications

All rights reserved.

ISBN: 0-9786944-1-4
ISBN-13: 978-0-9786944-1-8

To my mom, Doris. She has modeled love, grace,
and acceptance as a parent and friend.

To my Dad, Henry, who loves me
even when I do not check-in as I should.

To my Brother and friend, Charles, who inspires me
to be most noble in all my pursuits.

To my Bishop, Mary Ann Swenson, who encourages me
to lead and to speak in meaningful ways – for all God's children.

CONTENTS

ACKNOWLEDGMENTS

There are so many people who have contributed to this volume by way of sharing stories directly and indirectly; by inspiring me to study a text or to preach a sermon; by withholding information or by placing it all on the line. Most notably, my colleagues in ministry, lay and clergy, who face the challenges of each day by giving of themselves for the sake of the gospel, must be acknowledged.

I am deeply indebted to my closest friends for encouraging me. I also owe gratitude to my siblings, nieces, and nephews for allowing me to the space I need to be me. Regardless of where I may be in this world, all of you are near and dear to my heart.

INTRODUCTION

Every Thought and Prayer contained in this volume has been developed and birthed out of experiences in churches, malls, schools, Chapter meetings, conferences, and airports. Each Thought and Prayer has been crafted to challenge the reader to reflect upon his/her own experiences on life's freeways and side streets. Some issues may be reminiscent of back alley occurrences with chancel area implications.

My first book, "Thoughts on Things That Make You Think," was strictly a devotional text with word images and hints of a quest for divinity in this life and the next. Although there are some *favorites* from that book included in "Remix" fashion and noted by an "*", the core of Thoughts and Prayers are based more in the socio-political and spiritual milieu of our day.

I never want to be perceived as being overly political, but politics is a rudimentary reality for human beings because there is a system that governs our activity – inwardly and outwardly, as well as the influences we battle that are this-worldly and other-worldly. As a perceived spiritual leader among us, I must give voice to certain issues and concerns, not to control or direct the conversation, but more to the point of insisting conversation takes place. That is my hope I seek to actualize in this volume.

Thoughts On Kaua`i And Home

While serving as Guest Minister at The West Kaua`i United Methodist Church, I was reminded of home in so many ways. For those who know that I was born and raised in Alabama, that may seem like a far-stretch if you have never visited Kaua`i and rural North Alabama.

I grew up in a farm community, surrounded by family and extended family that had roots in that community. The name of the road that spans the community is "Bridgeforth Road" because ninety percent of the inhabitants on that road bear the Bridgeforth name and/or blood. When I was younger the road had some gravel sections and many driveways were mere dirt ruts in what was also the yard. From any point or from any homestead, you could look out in one direction and see the edges of the Tennessee River and in other directions, nothing but vegetation and forest. Well, when you could not actually see the River, you knew it was just beyond the trees and what I refer to as "forest" was known as "the woods."

No matter where you went in and around that community, you felt like you were somewhere special and you were special just for being there. My reflection upon that place now is much brighter than it was while I was experiencing it. That is probably because the problems I thought I had then were stepping stones and character builders that made me the man I am today.

My feelings while exploring the Hawaiian isle of Kaua`i had many elements that reminded me of home. The chickens and roosters all over the place was a clear sign that this was no ordinary place. People actually driving the slow speed limits through the towns and villages were a welcome surprise. Small churches in every community that seemed to sit at the center or in prominent places were also nice to see. Beyond that, the friendly faces and genuine hospitality shown in shops and in homes blew me away. The morning call of the roosters became a welcome sound after a few days. I really warmed up to them when I saw two of them sitting in front of the Starbucks. It was one of those moments that Kodak and Facebook are made for, but I could not get back to my car fast enough to retrieve my camera.

The people of the Church community extended warm hospitality to me at every turn and it was greatly appreciated. One invitation I received was to visit one of the members at the Kaua`i Care Center. I arrived at dinner time so I was not sure what to expect, nor was I aware of how I would conduct the visit while everyone was eating their dinner. The daughter of the patient and church member I agreed to visit greeted me at the parking lot and escorted me to the dining facility. As we walked into the room, she directed me to a table to the right where there were several people gathered, including some staff members. The daughter introduced me to her father and mother, one of her brothers, a church member, two nurses, two male patients, her mother-in-law, and we were joined by another church member.

After a few minutes of idle chat, the daughter suggested we sing and I follow that with a prayer. When we began singing "How Great Thou Art," those men and women who had seemed far from the conversation began to join in the singing. Others in the Dining Area also began singing along with us. The prayer I prayed was brief and it was followed by more conversation.

During our conversation I learned that one of the male patients was an avid harmonica player. It did not take much prodding to get him to retrieve it and bless us with a song. He asked, "What do you want to hear?" We said, "You decide. Play what you enjoy playing." He said, "OK! First, I will play this one."

He began playing the tune of "Yes, Jesus Loves Me," and we joined in. He followed with a Filipino folk song. While he was playing that one there was a woman who came over with her phone and held it up so the person on the phone could hear the harmonica. I am not sure of the significance or lyrics to the song, but it took them to a happy, happy place when they heard it. After the Filipino folksong he went right into "You Are My Sunshine." Again, those gathered joined in the singing. The visit had gone from a routine visit to a community event.

The singing and harmonica playing led to the other patient, who is the church member's roommate, to begin sharing that he was once a renowned trumpet and saxophone player. The female church member who was also their visiting said she remembered that her father played in the band with the man. When asked if he knew the woman's father, by name, he said, "Yes! He was my nephew." The daughter said, "This is his daughter." The man was over exuberant once he was given that information. It was reported that the man rarely spoke about anything, but here he was on that day singing and reuniting with family memories.

The reason I share this story is because it was while on the Island of Kaua`i that I was able to complete this manuscript, reconnect with God and nature and rediscover the true meaning of fellowship and family. It may be coincidental, but my visit spanned Holy Week and Easter. Many things that had been buried or lost were found and resurrected during my visit to Kaua`i and I shall forever be thankful for the experience and memory of home.

That is why the picture of one their two locations graces the cover of this book. Mahalo Nui Loa!

Thoughts On Why Me

Take delight in the LORD, and he will give you the desires of your heart. -Psalm 37:4(NIV)

Enjoy the LORD, and he will give what your heart asks.
-Psalm 37:4(CEB)

Have you ever stopped to ask yourself, "Why me?" Usually we ask that question of God when things are spinning out of control, we feel as though we are out of control or have lost control. But how often have you asked that question when things are going well and on schedule? Everyone is falling in line the way you direct. The funds are streaming in as expected. Relationships are putting smiles on your face. You could not imagine life being any better than it is...but, have you ever stopped in the midst of all of that goodness and asked, "Why me?"

"Look where he brought me from..."

During the summer of 1996 (Atlanta Games), I served as a missionary in Botswana. It is a country the size of Texas with a population of 1 million in Southern Africa. That was an experience that forever altered my life and my self-perception. It was while in Botswana that I discovered that there was a discipline of study termed black theology. I also learned to play chess. I learned that there is a snake in existence that can make small dogs disappear in a matter of just a few minutes. I learned that cheese, when it costs approx. $9 per pound is a delicacy. I learned that it is possible to get a haircut, under a tree, with clippers powered by the barber's car battery/generator. I learned that children, no matter where they reside are open, loving, accepting and curious. I learned that God is at work in so many mediums, religious expressions and cultures, beyond my own. All of those things were keen insights or expressions that enhanced my experience.

However, it was when one of the missionaries shared a verse of encouragement with me and the other 3 members of my team that my eyes were truly opened. The missionary began with the other male on the team and moved on to the 2 women. I was last. Mind you, the other team members received those well-known, cool verses (Jeremiah 29:11, Isaiah 41:9-10, Romans 8:28) that anyone would love to have spoken into their lives. The verse I received, with many prefaces was Psalm 37:4. I must have looked at the missionary with a puzzled look because her response spoke directly to my confusion.

THOUGHT: She said, "Don't worry about what you desire because God is the one who gives you the desires of your heart. But keep in mind that it comes as a result of you delighting yourself in the Lord."

God, let me come to know the desires you have placed in my heart. I want to rid of all selfish desires so that I can be a person of faith – one who loves you with my whole heart. I want you to forgive me for going my own way and acting out of selfish motives or power-filled ambition.

As you wash my heart and purge my mind, give me a drive to seek truth in your Word and find peace in your service. I desire to be a true worshipper. One who worships you in spirit and in truth. One who never doubts your presence or gives into the voices that speaks loudly of your inadequacy and irrelevance in my life.

I am a believer because you have given me grace to believe in you. I believe you are my heart's desire. And so it is!

Thoughts On Decisions

Do you have a difficult decision that you need to make? If so, keep reading. If not, have a wonderful day.

I have discovered that difficulty around decision making is usually related to or the result of the mystery that surrounds the decision. The "what if" game and the many in-head conversations you have with yourself that expose the litany of uninformed responses you may receive clouding the mind and blocking the heart from reaching any decision.

Here is something to think about: Don't let what you don't know determine your actions. Instead, allow what you do know to guide you. What do I mean by that?

You should know by now that God will never leave you and God will never forsake you. You should know by now that you have within you the very power that brought about resurrection on Easter morning. You should know by now that weeping may endure for the night, but joy comes in the morning. Those are things you know and can depend on. What you may not know is *how* God will honor God's word and presence in your life.

With such understanding you should know comfort, security, joy, peace, help, hope, faith and a future are yours.

THOUGHT: The lesson: you don't know what you don't know, so go with what you do know about the one who knows you best when facing tough decisions.

Lord, I know that you love me and that you only desire what is best for me. I ask you to help me grow in my understanding of you and your love. Also help me to wait upon you to lead me. Thank you for hearing and for answering my prayer. Amen.

Thoughts On Determination *

While waiting in a long line at the grocery store, I witnessed hope in action. Actually it may have been faith or just a wish that a stroke of good fortune would fall the way of the 10-year old boy who obviously had some financial backing for his project.

He was standing at one of those machines with the movable claw. He carefully inserted his bill and ever-so cautiously moved the arm over a Spider Man action figure and pressed the release. First try, no Spider Man. Second try, no Spider Man. Third try, he paused and walked around the machine to get a different view of his objective before trying again, no Spider Man. By now there are several other children gathered around in awe of what was taking place. The boy attempted a few more times, when suddenly one of the smaller children said, "Try something else!"

After the boy tried a few more times for Spider Man, he moved the arm/claw over just a smidgen' and finally secured a Power Ranger. I am certain I then heard the boy exclaim, "I just wanted something good out of there!"

THOUGHT: Sometimes we work to get the results we desire, with little or no result. We set in our mind that "this is it" and we move forward investing all the prayer, faith and resources at our disposal, when maybe our effort and intent are solid, but our actual goal or objective may be too much to bear. Or maybe our objective was set before us to get us in the vicinity of what we really need.

Lord, I have tried all I know to try. I have relied on the counsel of friends, the strength of prayer, and the truth that you know me and you want me to experience life abundantly. And so it is!

Thoughts On Being In God's Presence

When I first ventured into New Kingdom Church of God in Christ one Friday evening, I had one thing on my mind and one thing only. I was prepared and committed to attend the prayer service and proceed to Denver where I would enjoy my Friday night and Saturday morning. Somebody failed to alert the preacher of my plans. Someone failed to alert the architect who designed the building of my plans. But, as the service progressed, I realized that someone failed to alert my soul that it had grown empty and was disconnected from God.

The service began at 7:30pm and we did not emerge from the building until approximately 10:30pm, I still had time to get to Denver, but I did not have the drive or desire to get there. After hearing how much God had in store for me and how much responsibility I had as a recipient of His love, I felt overwhelmed, loved, and for the first time I felt responsible for something. I felt responsible for sharing the love of God with others. Once I realized that the love of God is not just something that comes and goes and that I have a part to play with moving it on to others, I had to rethink my priorities. I also had to reschedule my Friday activities.

After that experience, Friday nights were spent at New Kingdom and I looked forward to it.

THOUGHT: I cannot say that I never made it to Denver, but I can say that I never made going to Denver a priority on Friday nights.

Loving God, give me the determination, strength and passion I need to spend my time wisely and in service to you. I need you to help me find joy in spiritual things as I am transformed by the renewing of my mind. Amen.

Thoughts On Keeping An Appointment

I sat in a coffee shop waiting for my next appointment when I overheard a conversation between two women. One was a recruiter from a well-known business school and the other was a potential applicant. The recruiter told her, "Your credentials are impeccable. I appreciate you keeping this appointment, in spite of the bad weather we have been experiencing, but it shows me you are committed to your work and your education.

As the recruiter continued speaking, the candidate was rubbing her knuckles profusely under the table. The candidate was extremely nervous. Her nerves really got the best of her when the recruiter finally paused one enough to ask: "So, what other business programs have you applied to?" The candidate said, "Well, I uhm. I uhm...I applied to a couple local programs but that was really just to test the waters. Then I found out about how flexible your program can be, so I uhm...I decided to apply."

It wasn't the candidate's nerves, or the recruiter's tenacity that made this encounter memorable. It was the candidate's story that made it stick. After a few minutes of sharing in greater detail about the local programs she had applied to, she said, "As soon as I felt this program was the right place for me to be, things started to fall in place so it could happen. My husband works for the government, so prospects for him relocating from D.C. to Michigan were not in our immediate future without major sacrifice. However, I completed the application and continued praying about the possibilities. Then I learned of your visit to the area. The day I scheduled the appointment with you, my husband was granted a transfer to Michigan. With all of that, I know this is the right place and the right time. So, no matter how much rain was falling today, I was determined to keep this appointment."

The candidate went on for a while longer, followed by several exchanges with the recruiter. After the candidate was as candid as she was about her faith in the process and life, I was moved to tears. I thought back to times when similar things had happened to me and others, but I was also reminded of the many times that still, small voice had been silenced by reality and faithless chatter.

The recruiter shuffled through papers as they shared a little more. Then the recruiter said, "There were 5 other candidates who scheduled appointments with me for this morning, but all of them called, texted or emailed to say that due to rain, they would need to reschedule. I am impressed by your transcripts, work history and portfolio. I am also impressed by your story and your commitment, expressed by your presence here this morning...because you honored this appointment, I can guarantee your admission to the program."

You would have thought I had been admitted to the program the way my soul jumped for joy. There she was, as nervous as could be, but she was honest and committed before she entered the room. She did not shy away from the obvious hurdles of geography, personal financial challenges, her husband's employment, nor the rain. It was apparent she was a prayerful woman who had heard something deep within that gave her what she needed to pursue her dream. I guess that is why when I clapped for her, she looked over and smiled. The recruiter seemed annoyed that someone had overheard their conversation. Next time she will rent an office instead of meeting at Starbucks.

Help me, Dear Lord, as I seek to hear your voice and stay the course you have set for me. I pray that all chatter and clutter of my mind's eye and spiritual ear be replaced by markers of faith and peace as my soul says "Yes" to you and your will. Amen.

Thoughts On Rejoicing

The Apostle Paul was no stranger to adverse situations and chaos seemed to follow him or precede him everywhere he traveled. However, throughout the Pauline texts of the New Testament, we find him encouraging the Saints to be thankful and to rejoice always. What does he mean? How is this possible?

Be glad in the Lord always! Again I say, be glad! (Phil 4:4 CEB)

"Be glad" or "rejoice" means to express joy over and over and over and over and over...It does not refer to "remaining happy." Happiness is the result of an external stimulus or happening that makes you respond positively. Joy is the result of an inward working that cannot be explained, except that Joy is not determined by external circumstances or stimuli. Joy comes from God, through the Spirit.

Joy is based in your relationship with Christ. Will you express joy over and over and over, today?

When you are connected with God, you can have joy in the midst of chaos and you can express it over and over and over and over and over...and there isn't anything anyone can do to stop it – except you.

God, I have heard that "the joy of the Lord is my strength." If that is so, why do I feel so weak? Why am I not filled with joy? I feel stressed and anxious on occasion. I find it difficult to smile when all is falling apart around me. I desperately long to be me, yet I also yearn to yearn to be free to express my joy without judgment. Amen.

Thoughts On Trusting God *

When I was in college I was what they called a "starving student." I had to rely on God for everything. Things were so bad at one point that I went downstairs to get in my truck, which was on "E" to drive those 4 miles to school and found I had a flat tire due to a nail puncture. Under normal circumstances this would not have been a problem. I would have replaced the tire with the spare and moved right along. However, a week earlier I had to use that little donut spare and it was what was getting me to Friday.

I recall sitting there in the parking lot sobbing like a baby. I was scared, disappointed, and hopeless - you name it and I was it. Somehow I managed to drive that truck, with the flat tire to Big O Tire Center a few blocks away. I had gone through my change cups and had scraped the floorboard of my vehicle and had gathered a whopping $6.35, mostly in pennies. I seemed to have recalled a $5 spare tire sale sign at Big O...I drove in there and told them I needed a $5 spare put on and they said, "Aight." I sat there patiently, praying prayers of thanksgiving and singing little praises like, "*Great is thy faithfulness, great is thy faithfulness. Morning by morning new mercies I see. All I have needed your hand has provided. Great is thy faithfulness, Lord unto me*."

When the attendant came over and informed me that my truck was ready. I was getting ready for the embarrassing "clump" of all the pennies onto the counter when the man said, "That will be $18.20." He just as well told me the total was $5,678,234,987.19, because either way, I only had $6.35. So, I did what any other self-respecting person would do. I clumped my change onto the counter and began to count, "One, two, three, four, five, and six ..." and at about two hundred twenty-two, the man said, "Son, that one is on me."

Can I tell you that I suddenly knew what it meant to dance like David danced? What a day and what a way for God to again lead me through that *valley of the shadow of whatever that was* to a clear place of light.

Since that experience, I have learned that in order for there to be shadows there must be light somewhere. Even if it is in the distance and cannot be seen by the naked eye it exists. Many things we see in life are mere shadows of true realities.

We do not see things as they are. We see them through lenses of fear and doubt that have been formed over time through disappointment and despair. Sometimes what we see is smeared by our positive outlook on life and our need to see things as positively as possible. Regardless of the extreme lack of clarity we have, light is the necessary element that brings all things into focus. That day in the tire store, God used that attendant as a source of light. The pennies clanging on the counter were shadows of a reality that lurked behind the eyes and in the heart of a man willing to be generous to a starving student.

Great Creator and Sustainer of the Universe, thank you for providing me with what I need to be successful in life. I ask you to continue to provide me with what I need to bring glory to you and joy to others. Use me and where I am to be an instrument of light in the lives of others. Allow my presence and actions to call attention to how great you are and how marvelous life is in you.

When I focus on the shadows too long or allow them to become my reality, quicken my spirit and remind me that you are the source of light and you overcome all darkness in this world and in the one to come. Amen.

Thoughts On A McGriddle® *

I was very busy one day. It was one of those days when I had twenty-six hours of chores and errands to complete in a six hour timeframe. As I started my trek, I was "moved" to swing through a McDonald's drive-thru for a quick breakfast.

There I was in that drive-thru line trying to figure out what to order. I eventually settled on the Sausage McGriddle®. After completing my cash for breakfast transaction I proceeded to exit the parking lot. A black Ford Focus had stopped in front of me. I was slightly bothered by this because I think it is rude to block the flow of traffic just so you can check your bag for order correctness before leaving the lot. That should take place before leaving the window. So, there I am with an attitude and my attitude got even worse when I realized there was a Honda Accord in front of the Focus.

What I saw was a man on the driver's side standing with one foot in and one foot out of the car, while talking to a man who had his hand inside the passenger window. I was so bothered by this nonsense. My Sausage McGriddle® was getting cold, so I honked my horn. When I did that the driver of the Focus stuck his head out the window and yelled back at me, "Oh! I'm sorry; we should get out and help those guys push that car." I was embarrassed. The man in the Focus thought my honk was a request/insistence upon him to help the guys with the Accord, when it was really my insistence that all of them get out of my way.

THOUGHT: Anger and anxiety often blind us to reality. Frustration and haste cause us to miss out on ministry opportunities. Patience and love for humanity allows us time to look and the will to wait. But be careful because I was always told, “God stores patience on the other side of Hell, so you may have to go thru Hell to get it.”

Patience, Lord. Grant me patience, I think. Amen.

Thoughts On Living Past The Past

But she came and knelt before him. "Lord, help me!" she said. He answered, "It is not fair to take the children's food and throw it to the dogs." "Yes, Lord, but even the dogs eat the crumbs that fall from their masters' table."

-Matthew 15:25-27

In some ways, what you just read were scenes or acts that lead up to the climax or conclusion – it is what hooked you in, captured your imagination and kept you there until the end. At least that's how it happens with television and movies. Even in our lives sometimes we are captivated by our own or even other's past. We focus so intently on the past that it can keep us from seeing what we really want to see - the climax, the rescue, the plot twist, etc.

It seems that even Jesus almost got caught up in this woman's past, but the faith she had for her future, pulled him forward. Then Jesus answered, "Woman, you have great faith! Your request is granted." And her daughter was healed at that very hour. (Matthew 15:28)

THOUGHT: Life is like a show you have waited a long time to see that is different from what you expected, but you keep watching in hopes of a happy ending. Newsflash: Jesus died for you - HE has a happy ending in store for you, but you have to *faith your way* past the past. Do not spend too much time on it. Life is not TIVO. In fact, it's more like a 1 run, 1 act play that you never saw advertised - here today, gone tomorrow.

Lord, help me see others as you would have me see them. Also help me to see myself in a more positive light so I can vision past my own and others' pasts. I long to experience spiritual transformation in myself and in the lives of others. I am willing to let you lead me and guide me in your Word, your Work, and your World. Amen.

Thoughts On Giving Thanks *

One day while boarding the Metro in Washington, D.C., I witnessed the following: (NOTE: I will try to stay as true to the scene as possible and will provide names as to lessen the potential of confusing the characters)

Sherry was pushing her baby in a stroller, looking to ensure that she was boarding the proper train. As Sherry checked the train schedule, another train approached and Bomqueshia quickly disembarked.

Bomqueshia was also pushing a stroller. However, I wondered if Bomqueshia could read as well as Sherry because there was a very large sign above the escalator that prohibited several items and activities on the escalator - number one on the list was strollers.

As Bomqueshia began to disappear to the floor below, she yelled, "Sherry! Hey girl, you look good!"

Sherry looked up with a bright, delightful smile and said, "Hey! Call me. I got my cell phone back on! Yeah, that's right! That's right!"

Sherry continued pushing her stroller as Bomqueshia disappeared below responding, "Aight!"

In the moment I felt embarrassed for them. But as I rode the train into the city, I realized that what I was experiencing was not embarrassment for them. Instead, I realized that I failed to celebrate the little successes that come my way each day. For Sherry, having her cell phone back on was exciting and probably a great accomplishment - some might call it a blessing or a testimony. And Bomqueshia functioned much like a cheering section or an "Amen!" corner. They shared. They cheered. They celebrated right in my face, so I could hear it.

THOUGHT: Sometimes we can feed our own spirit when we challenge ourselves to see the success of each day. There will be negative aspects here and there, but surely those are not the sum-total of your existence. Celebrate the small stuff and "Amen!" others accomplishments along the way. Celebrate with others as they give thanks and praise for new horizons or opportunities. As we go throughout each day we are not fully aware of other's struggles or anxieties. We see people and take them at face value, or worse, we see little value in them at all.

Bomqueshia and Sherry were excited about what they could be excited about. We do not know what either of them was facing in their lives, nor do we know what was at work in their hearts. We do know that having the cell phone connected was important and a reason to celebrate. For others it may take purchasing a new outfit, a new car, a new home or winning the lottery to get the same level response. We just never know about those things, but we do know that it does not cost us anything to rejoice with others.

You are such an awesome God. You hear me even when I am not saying much of anything. You hear me when I say the wrong things and you do not scurry away when I do things that might otherwise create distance between us. You are steadfast and unmovable. I am in awe of who you are. I am grateful for how merciful you are. Your wisdom no one can fathom.

Give me the wisdom I need to see success in small accomplishments. Regardless of what I see or what others say, Lord, Help me celebrate who I am and what you are doing my life.

I realize that you are working things out for my good and that you only want good for me. Thank you for giving me good things to do, to be and to share with others. I especially thank you for awakening me more and more to the little things, so that the big ones do not overwhelm me too much along the way. Amen.

Thoughts On Courage

Be happy in your hope, stand your ground when you're in trouble, and devote yourselves to prayer. -Romans 12:12 (CEB)

When I was a child, one thing I hated hearing was "Boy, you are in trouble!" The announcement was usually NOT a surprise. I knew I had said, done or failed to do something at some time. Maybe I had gotten "out of line" at school... Maybe I said a naughty thing on the playground... Who knows? I hated being in trouble.

Trouble always came with consequences. Trouble always seemed to linger. Trouble always, or at least the news of trouble, seemed to travel swiftly and incorrectly.

What I find now is comfort in knowing that no matter who announces that I am in trouble, I am still a much-loved, cherished and protected child of God. Because I am a child of God, I know for certain that I am loved. I also know that "trouble don't last always."

THOUGHT: I am a child of God and there is not anything anyone can do to change that. I am created in the image of God and can strive to live into God's likeness. Think about it: Sometimes God [even] gets into trouble. People blame God for wars and for babies dying. People hate God when their parents get a divorce or a spouse is diagnosed with terminal cancer. People denounce their faith in God when natural disasters shake the social, political and spiritual fabric that has sustained individuals and communities for generations. So, sometimes people will hate me and they will not understand me, but God does, God always has and God always will understand me.

Give me the courage to say "No" to the things that others want for me, so I might begin to scream "Yes" to the calling you have upon my life. Amen.

Thoughts On The End of The Tunnel

I heard a comedian share once about being in a horrible situation. He had no idea how he would be able to pull himself together or to move beyond the mess he was in. He shared his plight with one of his closest and dearest friends. The friend offered a heartfelt, encouraging word. The friend said, "You've been dealing with this for a while. Can't you see the light at the end of the tunnel?" The comedian replied, "Yeah! But how do I know it is not a train?"

Sometimes we are so hard pressed with life and its issues that we are unable to even believe that there is a better, brighter or bigger "whatever" out there for us. But, that is a choice we make every day and in every situation. We determine how we will see the world and our plight. Jesus said, "The thief comes to steal, to kill and to destroy. I have come that you may have abundant life." (John 10:10). See, in that we already know the enemy's game plan. We already know our outcome. So, we can choose to focus on what the enemy is doing with the killing, stealing and destroying or we can choose to focus on the abundant life that Christ offers. Does this mean that the killing, stealing and destroying shall cease? No. But what it does mean is that your energies will be focused on the things that will overcome the evil, versus allowing the evil to consume your time and energy.

THOUGHT: You have a choice to believe if the light at the end of your tunnel is a train. You also have a choice to believe that it is the light of God letting you know that your labor is not in vain.

God, give me eyes to see the bright future you have in store for me. Grant me a spirit of optimism when looking ahead.

Help me rise above my own skepticism and cynicism so I might encourage myself and others. Amen.

Thoughts On Our Hiding Places *

You who live in the shelter of the Most High, who abide in the shadow of the Almighty, will say to the Lord, "my refuge and my fortress, my God, in whom I trust." -Psalm 91:1-2

As I child, one of my favorite games was hide-and-go-seek. I loved to play this game because it required creativity, agility and speed. However, the only time I remember playing the game and truly enjoying it was when we visited Mrs. Kathleen. She had six or seven kids and there were plenty more in the projects where she lived. It was like one big happy family - kids were always around and there was always a big kids' game in progress. There were several good hiding places and plenty of room to run when you were trying not to be apprehended by the chasers.

One thing that sticks out in my mind now is that although I was hiding, I was never alone. At least I never felt alone. It's as though knowing other kids were around, was my refuge. It's as though knowing that someone was always going to be looking for me and would eventually find me was my source of comfort.

Yet, as we consider hide-and-go-seek in a spiritual context, there is another side of this analogy that we must also address.

> *We aren't like Moses, who used to put a veil over his face so that the Israelites couldn't watch the end of what was fading away.* 14 *But their minds were closed. Right up to the present day the same veil remains when the old covenant is read. The veil is not removed because it is taken away by Christ.* 15 *Even today, whenever Moses is read, a veil lies over their hearts.* 16 *But whenever someone turns back to the Lord, the veil is removed.* -II Corinthians 3:13-16 (CEB)

Moses placed a veil over his face out of reverence for who God is. The Israelites "put a veil over their hearts," according to the Apostle Paul, which keeps them from knowing Jesus as Lord.

Hide-and-go-seek is what we play with God when we try to pretend to be something that we are not? It is the game we play with each other when we appear or pretend to be on cloud nine, when hell is where most of our mail is delivered.

THOUGHT: Maybe those early evening games of hide-and-go-seek are what have helped me to appreciate the love and life that God provides? God knows where we are at all times, yet the Lord pursues us with love and grace. The Lord knows when we are hiding, yet the Lord protects our lives and the plans He has for us. Hmmmm.....no matter how good my hiding place may be it is nowhere near as safe as the shelter of the Almighty, which trumps the mulberry bush behind Mrs. Kathleen's house.

Lord, I hope you are pursuing me. I pray that you come and that you find me in my hiding place. Rid me of all that I use to hide myself from you and from the world.

My soul hears you counting the seven days you took to create the world; the sixty-six books of the Bible you use to teach us; the forty-days Jesus spent in the wilderness you use to strengthen us; the three days he spent in the tomb you use to raise us up. My soul hears you counting so I can be ready to come out of hiding – in plain view of you and your creation – as you created me.

My soul hears you counting my sins as forgiven. My soul hears you counting on me to listen to you and learn from you. My soul hears you counting me as one in the number who will proclaim the triune God as my one and only God.

O God, I am coming out! Amen.

Thoughts On No Test, No Testimony

While stationed at Frances E. Warren Air Force Base, in Cheyenne, Wyoming, I attended New Kingdom Church of God in Christ. The energy level was a little different than it was in Oakville Methodist/Baptist churches of my homeland, but it was a good energy. I have several, vivid memories of how God moved in that little house where we met, but there is one that has to be shared today.

Every year Evangelist Molly Brown from Tampa, Florida would visit our Church. She wore very colorful outfits that always had matching, well "coordinated" gloves, stockings, handbag, shoes, handkerchief, and Bible cover. And there were those unforgettable hats. Sometimes I thought she had to sit down front with the ministers because her hats were too big to sit in the pews. [Back to the story] The last time I heard Evangelist Brown preach, she began with a song *"I haven't done nothing today, to make my Lord ashamed..."* Well, I could not sing that one that day because it was not true. But, her message was "No test, no testimony." Now that was not creative, clever or even original. However, it was directed at me.

THOUGHT: If I am to do anything great for God or in the name of God, then I have to know something intentional and personal about God. If am to speak of how God will make a way out of no way, then I have to experience that with God. No test, no testimony.

My Lord and my God, Thank you for letting me know that wherever I am and whatever I am going through, that my test will become my testimony. Amen.

Thoughts On Staying Connected to God*

The goal I pursue is the prize of God's upward call in Christ Jesus.
-Philippians 3:14 (CEB)

Sometimes when things that were once novel to us become familiar, they lose their flare and our attention often shifts to other places and things. This happened to us and to things we once cherished like an old doll, cool action figure, favorite dress, lucky cap, or special friends.

I share this because of a conversation I had with a person who stated, "I go to church almost every Sunday. I give an offering. I sing in the choir and I even usher and teach Sunday School when I have to. But, I just do not feel a connection to/with God. I try to read books to boost my spirit and to get me out of this slump, but nothing seems to work."

The person also shared that upon committing to be a follower of Christ that the relationship was the priority of that person's existence. This new-found salvation and freedom to love and to be loved was like a breath of fresh air. Now, that same relationship, with that same salvation and freedom seems burdensome and empty. That happens to many church people, but it does not happen to true disciples. Church people get sidetracked by 'church work,' but disciples focus on 'the work of the church.' Whatever tasks or ministries we find ourselves engaged in should point others and us to who God is and how God is at work in the world. Working with God is not easy, but it is not a burden either.

As the person poured out from the heart all that was in it, I was reminded of Apostle Paul's struggle to stay connected. He met opposition in many places and was ridiculed on every hand, but he knew that he had to do this one thing. This one thing would help him to prevail -- he had to keep pressing.

Pressing is like digging in, getting right next to, or even moving with force. Pressing is praying prayers and believing that God hears and answers them. Pressing is digging in your heels and daring the enemy to try to move your feet. Pressing knows that God is with you, even when you cannot muster up a feeling to contradict your current reality.

THOUGHT: We must "press" our way through the dry periods by praying for living waters to flow through our hearts. We must seek God to provide us with everything we need and consider what priority we place upon what we want. Those things God desires for us may only come through perseverance. If you can obtain anything on your own or of your own resource, then you do not need God's blessing or anointing in those endeavors. You are all sufficient. However, when you surrender your will for God's will, your way may not be easy, but it will be overcome as you press your way with the faith and hope that God is with you and God will make a way out of no way.

Give me strength and courage I need to press on and to keep moving toward the vision you have for my life.

When I am blinded by the light of temporary success, give me sight. When I am bound by my predictions and perceptions of others, give me liberty.

When I am convinced that I am not as good as everyone else, give me a reminder that I am made in your image. When I am confused about my identity, give me a reminder that I am a beloved child of God. When I fear, fail and fall, give me another chance. Amen.

Thoughts On Focus

To some who were confident of their own righteousness and looked down on everybody else, Jesus told this parable: 'Two men went up to the temple to pray, one a Pharisee and the other a tax collector... For everyone who exalts himself will be humbled, and he who humbles himself will be exalted.'

-Luke 18:9-14

The violent and destructive forces of Hurricane Katrina and Rita ravaged the Gulf States in 2005. The images of families trapped on roofs, huddled in neighborhood centers, rushing to nearby public arenas and flagging down any moving vehicle shall always be etched in my mind. Not only will those images remain with me, but so shall the accusations of neglect and conspiracy on behalf of the local, state and federal governments.

We may never know the whole truth of who was to blame for the devastating aftereffects of the storms. However, as we continue to wrestle with what has happened to devastate our gulf states, we must remain mindful of two facts. The first is that, finger pointing and name calling does not settle anything. In fact, such child-like behavior only serves to create greater divides and mistrust, which ultimately slows any potential progress. The second fact is that now is not the time to decide who is/was right or wrong. Suffering is wrong and as many still suffer, that is where all of our support should be directed -- economically, physically, and prayerfully.

THOUGHT: As you contemplate your thoughts on the matter consider this: God is not concerned with who/what is right as much as God is interested in whom/what is righteous.

Lord, I want to focus more on being righteous and less on being right. Help me release my ego, my anger, and my pride. Amen.

Thoughts On Desires *

Let the words of my mouth and the meditation of my heart be acceptable to you, O LORD, my rock and my redeemer.
-Psalm 19:14

When I was a child, I recall being told, "Watch the words you let come out of your mouth." At times I failed to heed that advice and was often scolded for such. I also recall being told that my mouth ought to be washed out with soap.

Words are very powerful. Words have the power to wound and to heal. Words begin and end wars. Words are used in wedding ceremonies and in divorce proceedings. Words bring us joy when they lead up to words like love and appreciate, yet words bring us sadness when they are surrounded by words like disappointment and hate. The words we speak can determine our next course of action or even the very pattern of our lives.

THOUGHT: No matter how powerful, interesting or damaging your words, what is more powerful is what you choose to meditate upon in your heart.

The anger, frustration and shame have not served me well. In fact, those things have held me back and reality is that I put those things there. Sure, experiences with others and my reactions to situations were catalysts but I chose to hold those emotions in my heart. It is unfortunate that many of my behaviors have been shaped more by those negative thoughts and emotions, while the Word and grace of God were present and available to me all-the-while.

Lord, create in me a clean heart, so that I may live and speak as you would desire. Amen.

Thoughts On Not By Sight *

"We walk by faith, not by sight." -II Corinthians 5:7

As I ran along the beach one morning, I noticed several interesting things. One thing I noticed was the lack of curtains on the windows of the homes that line the beach. Another thing I noticed was the number of individuals who were out there running, cycling, rollerblading and just sitting alone. Where had they come from and where were they going? What was the purpose of their presence in one of the most serene places in our region? An even better question: Why was I so concerned about their musings?

As I looked at various individuals I began to imagine why they would be out on a beautiful Tuesday morning, alone at the beach. Then I saw a man walking very slowly, alone with a cane. Surely he could find a sidewalk or a park close to his residence that would afford him ample walking space. I wondered why this man would struggle to cross the sand while walking with a cane when there were clearly easier routes he could have taken if all he wanted was some exercise.

Then, suddenly my mind went immediately to II Corinthians 5:7 (*We walk by faith, not by sight*). As soon as I arrived home I began studying that verse and came up with my own translation:

> *All of us, who endeavor to follow Christ, tread around with Christ, persuaded by Him instead of being moved by what appears.*

I have no idea why that man *had* to cross the sand but it appeared for him this was his goal and his only option. I have no idea how long it's been since he last saw the ocean. I have no idea if this is a daily ritual that gives him reason to live. What I do know is that he made his way to the edge of the water and he just stood there looking out toward Catalina. He looked more than content with his position and his accomplishment.

As I watched him I realized, we cannot afford to let what we perceive keep us from moving onward, upward or outward. We must tread around with the confidence that Christ provides, so we can stand anywhere for as long as we need to stand - without falling short due to someone else's or our own perceptions.

We must rid ourselves of the hopeless images that cloud our minds and fill our conversation. We must seek opportunities to be loving and kind in the world. We must. We can. We shall.

Lord, help me see beyond the horizon that others have set for me. Allow me to experience true, loving relationships with family, friends, and strangers. Allow me to extend grace to those who may not know you. Allow me to show mercy and compassion to those I know need it. Also, give me courage and faith beyond what I expect of myself.

Grant me new challenges that make me better, stronger, wiser. I desire to be better than I have been. I admit I act like I have it all together and that I do no wrong. But, you and I know better. You know the truth that is locked deep inside of me. You know my fears and my anxieties. You know how much I doubt myself and how much I really doubt you. Forgive me. Grant me additional chances to grow and to change. I want to be better, stronger and wiser in you, not of myself or in my own will. You are my God and I appreciate all that you do to keep me in this world, learning and loving, even with my limitations.

Thank you for your love. Amen.

Thoughts On Expectations *

As I ran along the streets one day I noticed the facial expressions of individuals who were walking their dogs, jogging, waiting at intersections, gardening and any number of early morning tasks. I noticed that some were smiling, while others were masked with blank stares into nothingness.

The thought that came to mind as I began to reflect upon what I saw was, "expectations." What expectations were those individuals taking into their homes, offices, relationships, and into their future? Were they expecting the absolute worse, without realizing that whatever horrible scenario they could have or always have concocted never comes to pass? Were they expecting the absolute best, hoping against hope that things would fall in their favor this time?

THOUGHT: Whatever expectations I take into any situation will have an impact on the outcome.

God, I need your guidance and intervention with regard to my expectations. I must recall times when you have moved beyond my limited thinking to make a believer out of me.

Help me recall times when you created something out of the nothing that I offered up for you to transform. I must recall times when I did nothing but you used me to make a difference. Help me recall times when I had given up but you continued cheering me on, anyway. I must recall times when you used my doubt to increase my faith or the faith of others.

Help me recall that I am supposed to help you help me by remembering that you are not limited by my limitations in the same ways that I am limited by them. Amen.

Thoughts On Envy *

Take delight in the LORD, and he will give you the desires of your heart. Commit your way to the LORD; trust in him, and he will act. He will make your vindication shine like the light, and the justice of your cause like the noonday. -Psalm 37:4-6

Envy is a feeling of discontent and resentment aroused by and in conjunction with desire for the possessions or qualities of another. Envy is one of those subversive emotions or states of reacting or being that eats away at us and our relationships [sometimes] without us knowing it. Envy will sometimes cause us to demonize others and make close friends seem like enemies. Why? Because they have something we want and/or think we deserve. We often do not think the other person is worthy. If we did, we would congratulate them on their success and work toward fulfilling our own destiny instead of hoping to catch a glimpse of theirs.

What is it about the way you were created that keeps you from being successful and believing in yourself? You may not be 6'2, with blonde hair and blue eyes, but you can be beautiful, if you look to become who God has destined you to become. You are beautiful. Since you were created in God's image, if you are not beautiful, neither is God. How absurd is that thought?

THOUGHT: The things you want for yourself or from others do not compare to the things God wants for you. The image you must use for comparison is not the one created by others. Look to the image God has in store for you.

Allow me to see and to seek what you desire for my soul, my heart, and my life. Amen.

Thoughts On Plans

"The plan is nothing; the planning is everything."

-Dwight Eisenhower

"Plans are only good intentions unless they immediately degenerate into hard work." -Peter Drucker

If we simply make plans but never implement them, then we place ourselves in a perpetual holding pattern. Plans can only be deemed valuable or useful after they have been implemented and evaluated. We have no way of knowing if driving directions will actually lead us to where we want to go if we never print them, get in the car, and start following the directions.

I realize that sometimes it is scary to think about striking out in a new directions or starting new ventures. However, at some point you have to move beyond the imaginary stage to the experimental stage (living and doing what you intend and hope to do). The latter requires faith, the former breeds apathy and limits your faith.

THOUGHT: Dreaming big dreams, living out of your own giftedness to achieve the greatness God desires for you will have you in places doing things you never thought possible. But, planning is only one step of this marathon called life.

Lord, help me to take my eyes off of others' prizes.

Center my focus on what you have for me. Grant me the strength and courage to accept what is mine and to work to attain what you have for me. Amen.

Thoughts On Listening *

Some time ago I attended one of those high-price, very nice affairs. It was one of those white linen table cloth, fine silver and dazzling crystal dinners, with who's who of Los Angeles in attendance.

As I sat there observing the comings and goings of some of the City's elite, I noticed that there were some who never actually occupied a seat; they just kept walking around table-to-table, greeting everyone. One of those "floaters" eventually made it over to our table. As she approached our table, one of the women at our table became overly excited about seeing the woman.

The woman walked over, kissed the ecstatic woman on the cheek, and politely greeted the entire table. After a few moments one of the men at the table asked the *floater*, "Did you work for Northrop?" As she stood erect and lifted one arm above her head in a Bette Davis-like pose, she said, "Work? I don't work. I am an heiress!" Everyone laughed. The man, pointing to his girlfriend said, "She must also be an heiress. She does not work either!" The girlfriend looked stunned as she said, "I am not an heiress. I am a Scorpio!"

THOUGHT: Funny? Of course it is. How often have you heard what you wanted to hear, answered a question that had not been asked or jumped to the wrong conclusion out of ignorance?

God, as I go through life, open my ears more and close my mouth even more often. Open my eyes more and close my mouth more often. God, open my plans, thoughts, senses and desires to what is right in you. Then, give me the words to speak, only if necessary. Amen.

Thoughts On Down, But Not Out *

Usually I resist sharing others' testimonies, but...

Philip was released from his second 3-day hospital stay within a two week period. After being released from the hospital near his former job, he decided he would stop in and share greetings with old friends and colleagues.

While he was waiting in the lobby, his old boss came out and said, "Why haven't you returned my call?" Philip asked, "What call? I have not been at work and I have been ill."

The old boss said, "Oh! Are you fine now? If so, I have a job offer for you.`What will it take to get you back? Philip said, "Honestly? A lot of money!" The boss smiled, "Be careful what you ask for."

After a two-hour visit, Philip departed the premises. On his way home he slipped into a nostalgic moment or two about days gone by at his old company. He remembered how supportive his old boss and co-workers had been when he first started the job. He shed a tear as he recalled his old boss giving him 2-weeks paid vacation while filing for divorce from his wife of 14-years. He almost had to pull his car off to the side of the road as he felt the love of his co-workers when he disclosed his sexual preference to them. Needless to say, Philip was having one-ole- emotional drive home.

Within a few hours the old boss faxed Philip an offer letter with compensation that far exceeded what he was receiving at his current job.

Philip arrived at his place of employment the following Monday with his new job offer in hand. He shared the letter with his supervisor who was furious, but said, "Don't do anything until you hear back from me."

So you can go on and shout, let me fast forward to the end of the story. Monday afternoon, remember this conversation started Friday; Philip was driving to work sharing his testimony with me. He remained at his current job, with a raise that exceeded his old boss' offer by 3%. The company reinstated his sick time and vacation time that he had used during his hospital stays, he has a permanent parking pass/space and he really feels appreciated by his employer.

THOUGHT: That is a testimony! What can we glean from Philip's testimony? God can bless you right where you are. You may not have to move to get the promotion or increase you think you need or deserve. Just because you are sick does not mean you are useless or without the hand of God all over you. Just because you are down now, does not mean you will be down forever. You may be down, but you are far from out! The Lord is at work in, for, through, and around you – working things together for your good.

At the end of our conversation, Philip said, "All I can say is, 'We must praise God in the midst of whatever we are going through because we do not know what He is taking us to or preparing us for…'but what we do know is that God is at work, even when we have not clocked in for a few weeks."

Lord, I believe you have my best interest at heart. Give me the strength and confidence to trust that even when I am late, you are on time. When I am absent, you are there. When I am sick, you are well. When I am lonely, you are present. Amen.

Thoughts On Forgiving Myself

If we say that we have no sin, we deceive ourselves, and the truth is not in us. If we confess our sins, he who is faithful and just will forgive us our sins and cleanse us from all unrighteousness.

-I John 1:8-9

What a wonderful gift – knowing that when we sin there is still hope. When we turn our backs on God and on each other, there is still hope. When we have no idea which way to turn, there is still hope. Hope is strength to keep going when you do not how the going will be but you accept that where you are going will be better than where you are – even if the "going" gets rough.

I must confess that I have done and said some pretty horrible and deplorable things in my life. I have acted out of malice and ignorance toward friends, colleagues and [even a few] church folks. I have known what Scriptures stated on matters, but willfully chose to act on my own intellect and lack of wisdom. I have missed many opportunities to right wrongs that I knew existed, all in the name of keeping peace and/or saving face.

The scriptures are helpful and full of hope because the words help us claim the truth and live out of a hope that comes from knowing that where there is sin, God responds with forgiveness. Now, if we could just learn to respond to our own sin and shame the way God does, then we might stop abusing ourselves and others so much when they get "it" wrong.

Lord, give me the courage to forgive myself and others for sins and acts that question or challenge our/my humanity and dignity. Allow me to accept forgiveness, but never to settle for the defeat that comes as I wallow in self-pity, self-loathing or pride. Help me say and accept, "I am a child of God and I am forgiven." Amen.

Thoughts On Personal Changes *

One Sunday I was standing at the back door of the sanctuary when a little seven year-old boy approached. The boy walked up to me, shook my hand and said, "Pastor, do people change?" I said, "Yes! People do change. Sometimes that's good and sometimes that bad."

He said, "My dad never changes." I said, "Yes he has – you just have not known him long enough to see it. Ask your mom. She has known him for a long time and she can tell you how he has changed since she has known him."

I am still not sure why he asked the question, but the question remains with me. However, I am also reminded that no matter how much people change – God and God's love remains the same. It is the constancy of God's presence that makes the "rollercoaster" emotions of friends and "valley-like" opinions of the world tolerable. Our existence in the world and our participation in God's transformative work are reflected in our attitudes and actions.

THOUGHT: The people in your home, family or office should see significant changes in your life, attitude or presence that helps them see or understand that God is with you and that God is with them.

God, thank you for this day and for this opportunity to extend thanks to you. Help me look to you that I may come to know what changes I need to make in my life and attitude that will bring me closer to you and to others. Help me down off the judgment seat so I can see people for who they are and not just for what I think about them. You look beyond my faults, so I desire to do the same for others. Amen.

Thoughts On Being Moved to Act *

...And yesterday, I laughed and laughed and laughed, until I cried.

Ellen DeGeneres, Cedric the Entertainer, Robin Williams, Bill Maher, Ray Romano and a few others stepped forward to salute HBO Executive Chris Albrecht for his commitment to mentoring. Chris comes from humble beginnings and remained committed to reaching back and reaching out to youth of all hues and challenges to let them know that they are not alone in the sometimes cruel world.

I sat there in the Kodak Theater and absorbed much of what the comics shared, but was most moved by the video clips that featured some youth and their mentors. Each youth spoke of his or her mentor as friend, confidant, motivator, encourager, and some even used sibling and parental language to describe the relationships. Nonetheless, the mentors and youths' lives have been touched and forever changed because of the relationship -- however it was described or experienced.

I sat there thinking that there are so many youth out there who need to hear the words, "I love you" or "you can do it." But who will utter those words to them? Who will love them enough to get involved? Who will be able to get beyond their own insecurities, wounds and misgivings long enough to share some life lessons with a youth in need? Who will gather the adult "have's" in ways that will allow them to share with the youth "have not's?"

A dear friend felt led to volunteer as a weekly reader at a local library. He signed-up for the program and he also went through the training and background check. By the time he had completed all of that, news of several local school staff being accused of harming children began hitting the airwaves. He contemplated for several weeks if it was worth putting himself in a position where he could be accused of something, or if he was going to trust what he had responded to initially. He grew up in a single-parent household and he knows the value of having positive role models and opportunities to get beyond your normal surroundings. The life he now enjoys as a productive, upstanding citizen is due to his family of origins investment in him, along with strong support from mentors and community organizations that encouraged him to strive to be the best at everything in life.

In our time of Priest scandals and local school teachers and staff being charged with sexual misconduct, it is a scary option to think: 1) Children are being taken advantage of by some in positions or authority; or 2) An accusation by a child could end your career and ruin your family forever.

After several weeks of deliberation, he has not assumed a volunteer position at the library. He wants to serve, but the cost associated may be too high for him.

Lord, help each of us find ways to be of service with those who can benefit from what you have done in and with our lives. I ask you to direct us to places and people who can and will inspire, challenge, and motivate us to share the gifts you have entrusted.

I also ask that you begin to work with us on how we can release our ego and pride in ways that will make us more approachable and acceptable within settings where there are opportunities to interact with persons who are not aware of what they need to do to be successful. This prayer is especially for men, women, boys and girls who fall victim to systems and constructs they did not create and do not know how to navigate – the sinner and those who have been sinned against. Amen.

Thoughts On Competition

Now I do this for the sake of the Good News, that I may be a joint partaker of it. Don't you know that those who run in a race all run, but one receives the prize? Run like that, that you may win. Every man who strives in the games exercises self-control in all things. Now they do it to receive a corruptible crown, but we an incorruptible. I therefore run like that, as not uncertainly. I fight like that, as not beating the air, but I beat my body and bring it into submission, lest by any means, after I have preached to others, I myself should be rejected.

-I Corinthians 9:23-27

When I was in 9th grade and my brother was in 10th grade we attended the same high school. Both of us played football but he was on the Varsity Team, while I was on the Junior Varsity Team. We were both very fast runners and were often compared to each other. We were very different in other ways. One of us were more astute academically due to natural abilities, while the other spent hours in study and devoted energy to memorization. One was keen on the notion of proving one's manhood by conquests of young ladies, while the other was more shy and unsure of him in that arena. One was outgoing in the religious sect of our lives, while the other was committed to a life of following Christ but did so through more subdued opportunities. As much as we were alike, we were different, except when it came to our speed on the field.

Neither of us really gave much thought to the comparisons nor to the idea that one was faster than the other. Well, we didn't until the day when both of our teams arrive on the practice field at the same time. The coaches spent a great deal of time discussing rather loudly which team would use the practice field. Finally, both coaches looked to the mob of players and summoned "Bridgeforth and Bridgeforth!"

I looked at my brother as he looked to his friends, smiled and made his way to the coaches. What we learned was that the coaches decided that the two of us would race and the winner would have full access to the practice field. Although there were many things going through my mind, I do not recall ever looking at my brother before that race.

We lined up, the coaches gave the signal and we were off! Neck and neck for the first 20-yards, but a nose hair of distance between us became apparent in the final 10-yards of the race. One Bridgeforth won the right for his team to use the practice filed that day. Another walked away smiling, sure he had accomplished something even greater.

Does it really matter who won that race? Does it really matter that one of us was slightly faster than the other? Who really won? Did anyone really win? [And] if so, what was won? If that is a valid question, I must also wonder what may have been lost, as well.

I am not sure what that little competition really meant or what overall or lasting impact it may have had on our relationship. However, we did what was asked of us – we ran the race.

It seems that this may be somewhat close to what the Apostle Paul is calling us to in I Corinthians. Paul began his journey to Damascus with one purpose in mind, but ended on a totally different trajectory. His life experience and pedigree assured him of worldly and ecclesial success and privilege, but God has a different plan. Paul would continue along his journey as one who would engage the work of the church, but in vastly different ways than he had had predicted. Paul ran the race.

The Apostle Paul may not have thought of himself as being ready for the leg of the journey chosen for him, just as my brother and I were not prepared for our race, but we had a particular race set before us, so we ran the race.

He mentions that we are all in a race, but only one receives the prize. That may discourage some, unless you realize that the "one" who receives the prize is not necessarily the first one to finish the race. The "one" who receives the prize is the "one" who completes the race. That is a distinction that must be made in this world. I am not sure Paul speaks of this in terms of what happens now when every child who participates receives a trophy, but maybe he is. After all, there is a certain amount of glory and pride that wells up within a person when s/he receives the trophy that is only fit for him/her and is based on his/her accomplishment. That may be one we could debate, but the point of the story is that each of us have our race set before us and we will finish it.

So, in the case of the race with my brother – both of us finished the race. And sometimes the prize others offer the winner is not the highest honor.

Lord, give me the strength to stay in the race. Grant me grace to celebrate small victories along the way, while resisting the urge to cheer at others shortcomings or failures. In moments when I act contrary to my best, remind me of times when I was not victorious and how I would have felt if others would have ridiculed me or reveled in my failed attempt(s).

*Also, help me share in others' joy, even when my own situation is bleak and I have little or no prospects of victory. Bring to my remembrance, your Word which affirms that "I can do all things through Christ..." (*Philippians 4:13). *Amen.*

Thoughts On A Conversation *

"For God did not give us a spirit of timidity (or fear), but a spirit of power, of love and of self-discipline." - II Timothy 1:7

I attended a public conversation between Al Franken and Ann Coulter. If you are not aware of whom either of these individuals are, then don't worry about it. If you are, then you are either rolling on the floor laughing hysterically at the mere possibility of what might have been spoken. Or, you may be sitting in awe, wondering if such a conversation was productive.

Al and Ann are both authors and political commentators, of sorts. Basically, Ann is conservative; Al is liberal. Ann supports the war in Iraq; Al supports ending the war. Ann responds with short, concise answers; Al responds with long, drawn out answers. Ann was not interested in talking about herself; Al shared his thoughts about himself, his heroes, his family and he shared many thoughts about Ann.

Overall, the presentations by both commentators were interesting, yet boring, all at the same time. The Question and Answer session was more like a brawl than a debate. The audience offered visceral responses to comments made and ignored by both presenters. I sat there wondering what I might share [with others], of interest from the 2 hour presentation...

A person or group becomes an enemy when you decide that you will not tolerate their opinions or actions. They become an enemy when you decide that you do not like them. They become an enemy when you decide their human dignity and worth are part-and-parcel to your thoughts and feelings about the position or views they espouse. Your enemies are created by you. People and groups do not decide to become your enemies; you determine them to be enemies based on your own criteria. They can be your enemies, even if they do not wish to be so because you are in control of who your enemies are.

As I listened to Al and Ann, it was clear the goal for the audience was for them to listen. After-all, it was a speaker's series. That meant the audience was assembled to listen to the speakers. Not to ignore one or the other, but to listen to what the speakers had to say. The key is to listen. That is what makes free speech worth anything – the freedom to speak and to be heard.

Oops! I almost forgot. Do not become angry with a person for being bold, courageous or even shallow enough to share their opinion. Do not grow weary because you are afraid to share your opinion – do not hold others accountable for your unwillingness, inability and/or fear of speaking out. Free speech is costly.

Lord, I want to listen with my ears and respond from my heart. Allow me to be more like you are when I pray. You listen intently to what I say and to what I do not say. You are patient with me when I go my own way and when I have thoughts that are contrary to yours. But you do not close my access from you. In fact, you seem to bring me in closer when we are not in agreement. That allows me to hear you, see you, feel you and follow you in more authentic and intentional ways. That would not be possible if you pushed me away or shut me out whenever my thoughts were not in alignment with yours.

Grant me the courage and strength I need, to be the bold and courageous disciple that you have called me to be – listening and loving as you do. Amen.

Thoughts On Love Thy Neighbor *

The foremost is...you shall love the Lord your God with all your heart, and with all your soul, and with all your mind, and with all your strength.' "The second is this, 'You shall love your neighbor as yourself.' There is no other commandment greater than these.
-Mark 12:28-31

I was driving hurriedly and ended up behind someone who was truly out for a Sunday drive. It seemed that everything was working in that person's favor. My first response was one of disgust because if that person had driven a little faster I would have also made the lights.

Well, as some Sundays go, I parked in a nearby parking lot, tended to my business and prepared to return home. Wouldn't you know it...that car that had caused me such grief was leaving that same parking lot, traveling in the same direction. Now I was really getting bothered. How was it that I was being hindered by the same car twice in one day?

I meandered back along Coliseum behind the little white Honda. Whenever I needed to make a right, so did the Honda. The funny part of this is that when I signaled to turn onto my street, so did the Honda. Now I am really laughing.

When I signaled to make the necessary U-turn to get to my home, so did the Honda. Can you see me stuck somewhere in the middle of the twilight zone? The Honda made the U-turn and so did I. The Honda passed up two buildings and parked on the street. I thought, "at least you are not blocking my driveway."

I parked in my garage and as I walking up to my apartment I saw the woman as she yelled, "Hello! You must be my new neighbor. I was planning to stop by to introduce myself later today but since we are here…my name is Cheryl."

We stood there on the sidewalk exchanging niceties for a few minutes. I felt bad for thinking such horrible thoughts and for drawing such negative conclusions about this woman's evil plot to destroy me and my Sunday afternoon with her driving tactics. We completed our conversation and as I walked away I looked down and noticed that Cheryl was wearing a very large knee brace.

Of course I wondered why she would put herself in danger by driving in her condition, but then I remembered one thing Cheryl said during the course of our conversation. She said, "I just moved to California a few months ago and I do not have any family here."

THOUGHT: What kind of neighbor am I? Do I really love my neighbor? Here is a woman who is miles away from family risking her life and the lives of others to get a few items at the pharmacy, but I was so focused on my disgust that I completely overlooked any needs that Cheryl may have had or expressed.

Dear Lord, help me to love myself and to cherish life so much that the mundane things of this life do not hinder me from also loving my neighbor. Help me to extend hospitality in this hostile world. Help me recognize what it must feel like to have to adjust to a new way of being – among strangers.

You created us to be in community and to care for each other. You created us to love each other. In fact, as you spoke to your disciples at the Passover, you said, "they will know you are Christians by your love for one another." Your love is my love. My love is for my neighbors - all people. Amen.

Thoughts On Showing Love *

See what love the Father has given us, that we should be called children of God; and that is what we are. The reason the world does not know us is that it did not know him. Beloved, we are God's children now... -1 John 3:1-2a

Once, while visiting with a dear friend and her family, I noticed how much love, grace and patience with others, particularly children, can pay-off in the long run.

The couple has three little children, a boy and two little girls - twins. The little boy is at the age where he is getting into everything; he watches your every move and hears your every word. His eyes are big and beautiful and are filled with joy and wonder as he moves about the house.

I watched him pick-up his toys as he moved them from one room to the other – he was very careful with all of his items. Even when he approached the household cat and dogs, he was very gentle with them. At one point I said to the father, "He is very careful and almost nurturing with all of his things...even the way he interacts with the animals demonstrates some kind of affection and admiration."

The father responded, "It only works because the feelings are mutual."

It took me a minute to slip into reflective mode, but I did and I quickly realized that the little boy had figured out what many adults need to figure out – for love to be beneficial and efficacious it has to be mutual. Otherwise, we feel that we are taken advantage of or that we are wasting our time loving someone who will never love us back.

That little boy expressed his love for those animals and they expressed their admiration for him – their relationship worked beautifully. Just imagine the potential damage that could result if one, the boy or the animals, changed their opinion toward the other...disaster, disaster, disaster.

The thought of what this little boy is modeling for his younger sisters is also important. But, where did the boy learn this behavior? How did he figure it out?

Our parents, friends and general community teach us many things about how to be in harmonious relationships. Sometimes harmonious existence comes by way of silence and compliance and other times it comes as a result of open and honest communication.

When silence and complicit behaviors are favored or rewarded it teaches us how to be quiet and allow things to happen in us or to us that we may not appreciate. However, over time it becomes our norm and whenever we hear or see something contrary to our way of being we struggle to make sense of it and may even avoid it out of fear for what may happen to us if we act or respond that way.

Love calls for action, communication, and expression of one's true self. Love calls for exploration of what it means to have voice and liberty in the world and in relationships. Love never fails. Things that we refer to as love or believe is love, succeed when there is mutual participation, understanding, and adherence to the established norm that is not God's norm, nor is it healthy.

God, you created me out of love, to love. Help me move beyond relationships that are not steeped in or built upon love. Help me give and receive love with gladness. Amen.

Thoughts On Waiting

Wait. Be Patient. Stand still. Who needs it?

Waiting just gives you time to think of other things you could be doing instead of waiting.

Patience makes you seem helpless and standing still gives a sense of inactivity or motionless.

However, imagine sitting in your living room waiting for a visit from someone you deeply love, honor, respect and care for deeply, who promised to visit. What are thinking while waiting? Does patience seem to be a hindrance? What if you left the house only to return to find that the visitor had stopped by while you were out?

Much of what we are called to do as Christians can be found in this scenario. We are awaiting the return of the Messiah. We wait to hear his voice say to us each morning, "Arise!" We wait to hear him give us direction in many areas of our lives. We wait to feel his touch. We wait to return to him.

THOUGHT: As followers of Christ, we will not go or tread in any place that He has not first ventured into or beyond. Patience becomes a tool for our benefit, not a guise to strip away our sanity. We must stand still so God can position us to receive, to hear, to see and to feel the Messiah as he comes to us each day and in so many ways.

Deliverer, Sustainer, Comforter, Savior, and Lord, please continue to give me what I need to be able to do what I need to do for your glory. Even if it means I must exercise faith and patience while you do your work in me. Amen.

Thoughts On Forgiveness

Then said Jesus, Father, forgive them; for they know not what they do. And they parted his raiment, and cast lots.

-Luke 23:34

If what Jesus endured and demonstrated on the cross is to mean anything, then we have to dig deep, like Jesus, and do the godly thing [not the easy thing] and forgive those who seek to destroy or demean us. Also, we must understand that forgiveness is not synonymous with forgetting or moving forward together.

Forgiveness is acknowledging that someone has wronged you, but knowing that your heart is too precious to hold anything evil, you release the thoughts of vengeance and wrath, allowing love for God and humanity to prevail be saying, "I release you and I let go of my hard feelings." This does not mean that your standing lunch appointment must go on as usual. Instead it means that your relationship can move on, even if that means you two are no longer in the same type of relationship you were in before the infraction. Forgiveness is moving beyond the wrong, releasing the harshness from your heart.

THOUGHT: Knowing that Jesus was willing to forgive those who were determined to kill him is only beneficial if we are willing to follow his example, while also acknowledging that we often require forgiveness for ourselves. If we have not deposited any forgiveness, then we should not be sad when we find that our "forgiveness" account is empty.

Lord, grant me the ability and the willingness to release the harsh feelings I hold toward others. Give me courage to speak forgiveness more than I seek forgiveness. Amen.

Thoughts On Mr. McGregor

Mr. McGregor owned a little neighborhood store near my grandparents' home. When we would visit my grandparents it was always a treat to skip down the path that led to Mr. McGregor's store. I believe cookies were 10 cents and there were these huge jugs of what we called penny candy. Mr. McGregor always seemed happy to see us. In retrospect, I think he was happy to see everyone who entered his store. I can recall being in there one day. Mr. McGregor gave me a little brown paper bag and said, "Fill it up."

I looked at him with surprise and fear in my heart and mind. I only had a quarter to spend. I told him about my "economic" situation, to which he replied, "Someone wants you to know how good it feels to fill up a bag full of candy. Go ahead!"

I hurried as I filled that little bag. I placed my quarter on counter spoke a word of thanks and headed for the door. He yelled to me, "You're welcome! But someone else paid for that candy- I didn't."

THOUGHT: To this day I have no idea who wanted me to know the joy that is seemingly only important to an eight year-old. However, the last time I was in Hartselle, Alabama, I drove past what used to be Mr. McGregor's store and it was good to recall that moment, because the experience also connected me with thoughts of God and how God manages to take care of certain situations before we even arrive - just so we can know the joy of knowing that someone is working things out for our good.

God, thank you for tending to the little things in life, so that we can perceive and receive them as big blessings that make our lives and our world better. Your kindness shall be magnified. Amen.

Thoughts On Praising God

What do you do when you have poured your heart and soul into someone, expecting some growth or fruit to show in return? What do you do when you have loved as deeply as you know how to love, expecting a little sentiment in return? What do you do when you have moved to a point where you are willing to die for another, expecting them to simply acknowledge that fact? What do you do when you have made yourself available 24/7/365, expecting to be acknowledged at some point? Yet…you wait…?

I suppose that such questions remain on the heart of God as God reflects upon all that has been put in place through the ages to extend love, grace and mercy to humanity. God has gone to great lengths to show humanity ways of being good and decent in this world, expecting the good that has been given to be shared with others. In a world where people hunger and thirst for basic necessities while other are not innocent of indulging in guilty pleasures, great pain and suffering will exist. Great divides between the haves and have not's will continue to increase. Feelings of neglect and entitlement will become the norm.

The whole of the Gospel and the yearning of the hearts of those who want to be better and experience more *good* in the world call for a spirit of generosity and praise.

Generosity is expressed by those of give of their resource; whether they have measurable wealth or an abundance of prayer they give it away. They give it, not expecting it in return, yet it comes to them. It comes to them because they have made room for it – they can receive it because it has been given to someone else who can in turn give it unto them. The same is true of praise.

When praise is received it can be offered and received again. That is why it important to praise God and to praise individuals for the contributions and enhancements made to your life and existence. It is equally important to offer praise as it is a clear indication of your ability and willingness to take note of activities and challenges around you that prompt you to do more and/or to be better than you have in the past. With God, praise is an acknowledgment of your awareness of His great gift(s) to you. As you recognize God's greatness, you come into an understanding of your own ability to do and to be great in the world. As you live into that greatness, you make room for praise to come your way.

Sometimes as we acknowledge the presence and power of God at work in us and in the world, we become more aware of our own shortcomings. We begin to see how often we miss the mark or "fall short of God's glory" (Romans 3:23).

A very dear friend told me of an incident in his life when he was brought face-to-face with his own frailty. Some would say, "he became acquainted with his own demons." He was at the top of his career. He held few heroes in his heart and life, but he was hero for scores of professionals who knew him as healer and as a trusted friend and colleague. In his mind and in the hearts of others he could do no wrong. The world was his to own and to direct as he so chose – based on his impeccable character in his professional and personal arenas. He was a devout churchman who gave of his time and talent to improve the spiritual experiences of others. Again, he could do no wrong, as he was at the top of his game.

One day as he was going about his life, being the envy and goal of many, he had a lapse in judgment that he, his colleagues, his community, nor his family saw coming. He believed his own hype.

He bought into the notion that he was "the man." As "the man" he made a decision to live out of the clout he had en massed at work and in the world to make an unwanted and unwarranted advance that could have cost him everything.

As he reflects upon that phase of his journey, many years later, he can see how he failed to give credit where credit was due. He can see how he failed to acknowledge God in all of his ways. He can see how he believed that being deemed the best by others; he believed he was the best.

He may have been the best at his profession, known for his community engagement and begrudged for his family life, but he lacked the ability to praise God and to praise others for their contributions to his success and development. He did not intentionally dismiss people.

He did not use demeaning speech in relation to others, but something about the *power* and *success* of his life's portrait seemed eternal and impermeable. But, when others were not looking he made a grave error because he relied more on his own strength and perspective to uphold his positions in the world than he relied on God – the one who had gifted him with what he needed. But God was not the one relied upon when "test time" came to his front door.

This principle is one that can be applied in most aspects of our lives and our being. We give praise and opportunities to others, thereby, making room to receive praise. Not to fill our heads with vain glory, but to bring us to a place where we realize we are who we are and where we are because of whom and where God is.

It is God who gives and takes away. It is God who waits to be praised for who we are and for who God is in our lives. When we praise God – offer thanksgiving – we become more aware of how limited we are in and of our own selves. We can do nothing great and lasting without reliance on the power than can come only from God.

My friend prayed and thanked God on a regular basis, as many do. But he missed the fact that he was not as great as other thought he was. He was greater because the image God created him in was far greater in detail and substance than he or anyone else knew. Today, my friend reflects upon his experiences and is clear that he is a child of God.

He is clear that God made him and God is the one who sustains him. He praises God not only for where he is, but he praises God for being a mirror unto his own life and the lives of others. He praises God for bringing him through his difficult season where he could have lost it all to a point where he "counts it all joy" (James 1:2).

God I love you and I believe you love me. I no longer desire to resist your love. I no longer desire to ignore your grace. I no longer desire to deny your mercy.

However, without my resistance, ignorance and desire, I am void of a familiar way of being in this world. I have been selfish and self-absorbed, so I need you to help me to serve, love, and give to others so I can be all you have called me to be.

Help me see areas in my life where I am holding on and holding back personal, emotional and economic resources that could be used for greater good of others and me.

In the meantime, give me something to do while I trust you to work for my good, while I prepare to do well in the world.

In the meantime, give me a greater understanding of who you are and who you desire for me to be.

While I wait, build me capacity to trust you and to trust myself to trust you more. Build my capacity to love and to cherish each moment I have to be made over. Guide my thoughts and control my heart because I have not done a very good of either.

I know you to be loving, kind, merciful and gentle. I know you to be my God. So I will wait with and for you, my God, to will and to do all that is good and perfect in my heart and life.

I also lift up my friends and family - those who are struggling through their experiences, unaware of the blessing that awaits them. Just as my friend made it through his difficult period, they can make it through theirs. But they may not know how good you are.

They may not know you are working things out for their good. They may not know that weeping endures for a night, but joy comes in the morning (Ps 30:5).

They may not know that you will never leave them, nor will you ever forsake them (Hebrews 13:5).

They may not know, you came that they may have abundant life (John 10:10).

So, in the midst of my asking, I also ask for strength and courage to share my own testimony, so they may come to know how good you and perfect you can be in their hearts and lives. Amen.

Thoughts On Honoring God

Now when the Pharisees and some of the scribes who had come from Jerusalem gathered around him, they noticed that some of his disciples were eating with defiled hands, that is, without washing them... 'This people honors me with their lips, but their hearts are far from me; in vain do they worship me, teaching human precepts as doctrines.' You abandon the commandment of God and hold to human tradition...Listen to me, all of you, and understand: there is nothing outside a person that by going in can defile, but the things that come out are what defile." (Excerpts from Mark 7:1-15)

Jesus challenges the dietary laws and the contradictory nature employed by the religious establishment that allowed them to alter the Law to satisfy their own way of life and thought. He called them hypocrites who spoke of godly things but their lives had no manifestation of holiness.

He noted the words of Isaiah that said, you "honor me with your lips but your hearts are far from me." Jesus is challenging what they call worship. He is admonishing them for calling *lip service* worship. He is admonishing them for teaching human doctrines as God's will and way. Ultimately, if we were to look at what Jesus is setting up here we would see that he is writing a prescription for worship.

Worship is a space and attitude that honors the Lord with our hearts. Let what glorifies the Lord come from our heart, not from your lips. Worship is not defined by music or liturgy. Worship cannot be confined by brick and mortar or the ticking of a clock. Worship takes place in the hearts and lives of those who honor God. Worship takes precedence over all else in the life of a disciple of Jesus Christ. Worship is a means, not an end to a devoted and sanctified life.

To be devoted is to place the reverence and relationship you have with and for God at the fore of thoughts and activity. To be sanctified is to be set aside for God to use as God desires, when God desires, in the many ways God may choose to use you. You can decide to be hypocritical or apathetic when it comes to worship. You can decide to make it about the outward expressions or emotions, but where will God be encountered? Is God glorified by your feelings?

God calls for expressions based on pure love, not words coming in response to fulfillment of a human doctrine. Worship is based on total surrender to the Word, will, way and presence of God. Worship is not about the music someone else is rendering, it is about the song you sing to God each time you offer praise and thanksgiving, which may be marked by seemingly chaotic rhythms or utter silence. Both are equally as powerful responses to the Lord's awesome presence. Worship is not about your feelings because Worship is not about you. It is about God!

God, transform me from this spirit of 'me' to a spirit of 'you.' Help me let go of what I want and begin to praise you and thank you for what you provide, which is exactly what I need. Help me offer myself and my words as sacrifices to you all day, each day. Help me realize that worship must be at the center of my life and thoughts far beyond Sunday morning.

When I am able to allow you to work in this way, then my spirit will point toward 'you' and on 'me.' Besides, that's your job. Amen.

Thoughts On Being Strong

And that about wraps it up. God is strong, and he wants you strong. So take everything the Master has set out for you, well-made weapons of the best materials. And put them to use so you will be able to stand up to everything the Devil throws your way. .. This is for keeps, a life-or-death fight to the finish against the Devil and all his angels. Be prepared. You're up against far more than you can handle on your own. Take all the help you can get, every weapon God has issued, so that when it's all over but the shouting you'll still be on your feet. Truth, righteousness, peace, faith, and salvation are more than words. Learn how to apply them. You'll need them throughout your life. God's Word is an indispensable weapon. In the same way, prayer is essential in this ongoing warfare. Pray hard and long. Pray for your brothers and sisters. Keep your eyes open. Keep each other's spirits up so that no one falls behind or drops out. (*The Message,* Ephesians 6:10-18)

The King James Version of this text reads, "*Be strong in the Lord and in the power of his might*" (v10). I first heard this verse as a young man, growing up in a rural church in Alabama. I recall hearing the preacher scream, "Be strong! Hold on! Stay in the race! Don't give up! God's got...every...thing...under... control!

Although I appreciated the fervor with which this message was delivered, I was confused about what any of that had to do with my ability and my call to be strong. What I have since learned is that the greatest strength I have or ever can have is that which comes from relying [fully] on the Lord. I must place even the minor decisions and considerations before the Lord. I confess, I often take care of the little ones and call on the Lord for the things when I need back-up. Although that may seem reasonable, it really diminishes my perspective of who I am and what the Lord really is capable of doing in my life – now and in the future.

If I really want to be strong in the Lord, then I have to let the Lord exercise the Lord's strength to heal, forgive, deliver, restore, transform, direct, redirect, etc. It is in the ongoing interaction and partnership with the Lord that I come to know the Lord's strength. Whenever I begin to think I can accomplish this or I can do that, I in effect, make a declaratory statement that I do not need God.

If anything can be accomplished without God, then it does not require faith. If anything can be accomplished without acknowledging God, then it does not belong in a testimony. Such things belong on a 'brag sheet' that marks one's victories. However, testimonies are made of hard work and reliance on the wisdom and presence of God. A true testimony is not about what happened, but it's about what God did to make the new happening.

The text admonishes us to "Be strong in the Lord!" By relying on the Lord to be Lord in our lives we will be strong! Hold on! Stay in the race! Don't give up!

God, give me the ability to let you work in every area of my life. I am not always open to your Word or to your way of working, but on some level I know it is best. I struggle with letting go of control and allowing you to take over.

My faith is not that strong yet. Allow me the comfort in knowing that you are capable of making miracles happen in big and in small ways.

Allow me to fade to back and you take center stage in my life. I love you for the love and care that you extend, whether I thank you for it daily or not. Amen.

Thoughts On A Trophy

When I was in high school I weighed approximately 125 pounds and I was a sprinter on the track team and a running back on the football team. I like to believe I was quite the athlete. During my Junior year I entered a weightlifting competition in hopes of winning.

I signed up for the "Under 140 Division" because I thought that was for individuals who could lift less than 140 pounds. As things progressed it did not take long into the competition for me to realize that the 140 pounds was in reference to MY weight. What a surprise! Being the dedicated soul that I was I did not withdraw from the competition. I managed to lift everything my competitors could lift until finally we were down to two of us remaining in my division. The other guy was little stockier than I was and he was known to be much stronger than he appeared. We lifted the same, pound for pound, through 3 or 4 more rounds, there was no way either of us were going to just give up.

How many times have you found yourself in a competition that you knew in your heart you had to win? It did not matter how great the odds or the challenge, you just knew in your heart that victory must be in your future? The Apostle Paul challenges you to "let the mighty strength of the Lord make you strong."

Let all that God has ordained for you give you strength in knowing that the Lord holds your future just as the Lord has held your past. Let all the victories God has brought to pass before, give you strength in knowing that what the Lord did once, the Lord can do again. Let all the love God has shown you give you strength in knowing that you are the apple of the God's eye, even when others are blind to that truth.

Let the simple fact that God has gifted you with everything you need to accomplish every goal and you have strength in knowing that the Lord will see you through every trial and temptation to ensure that you have a testimony at the end of your test.

All you have to do is surrender your own will and power to God's will and power. All you have to do is let God be God, let God stand at the center of your heart and life and that will give you the strength to stand. Why? If God is standing at the center, then you cannot occupy that spot. If you allow God to lead, then you do not have to worry about leading. If you allow God to speak, then you do not have to worry about not having the right words. If you allow God to be God, then you don't have to be in charge of your own destiny any longer. God will handle it.

I was not fully aware of Ephesians 6:10-17, during my Junior year, but after our division was down to only 2 of us, we lifted the same, pound for pound, through 3 or 4 more rounds, there was no way either of us were going to just give up. Finally, the Coach said, "Tell me the maximum you think you can lift and we will see if you can lift it. If you can and your opponent cannot, then you win." The Coach turned to me and asked for my maximum. I told him I could lift 205 pounds. The Coach turned to my competitor and asked for his maximum. He said, "I can lift all that the Lord allows me to lift. So put 205 on there and let's see what happens."

The Coach mounted 205 on the bench and I began to pray because my competitor spoke words that reminded me that I could do all things through Christ who gives me strength. My competitor went first. He struggled but he was able to lift the 205. I stretched out under that bar and continued to pray, "Lord, give me strength." I managed to lift the 205 and feared trying any more than that. However, when the coach asked my competitor if he wanted to go up to 210 or 215, he answered, "I believe the Lord has determined that 205 is my max. I am not willing to go any higher." That meant he forfeited going forward to another round and I, by default, took the coveted FIRST PLACE trophy.

There are several lessons in the story. One is about knowing when God is speaking to you and knowing how to discern your proper response to the message. Sometimes our lives are so crowded or our egos are so large, we cannot hear God's voice, nor can we see what God is doing in us or others.

God may be telling or showing us we have come to the end of our abilities and it is time for God to take over or God may be showing us an ending that will mark a new beginning in a completely different direction.

If we do not pause, listen and render a careful and thoughtful response, we may advance beyond our capacity and/or God's calling upon us. Both are dangerous, but God can and God will work with us through those circumstances to make us stronger.

Another lesson is that God is always present and able to help you. Just as the other competitor relied on God's leading, I had to do the same. By doing so, both of us were spared embarrassment that could have come as a result of us acting on our own volition and being driven by our desire to win. Is that to say we were two spiritually astute teens? Of course not! But, God used that situation to teach both of us a valuable lesson about listening for the Lord's voice and trusting in the Lord's presence to aid us in times of need.

Yet another lesson is that when you are committed to doing what God has gifted and commanded you to do, do not give up unless that is what God has told you to do. Why? My victory in that competition was just as much about somebody else knowing their physical and spiritual limitations as it was about me trusting God to advance me in the competition.

That is not to say God is in the business of answering prayers that cause any one of His children to think less of them when an award or accolade is not conferred upon him or her. God wants to be with us in our triumphant and victorious moments just as much as we want God with us when we are struggling and in distress.

Our ability to open up to God when we know we need God and when we consciously or subconsciously do not realize we need God is a measure of our growth and understanding of God.

Thank you, Mike...I really wanted that trophy. It gave me a boost of confidence, but it also catapulted my ego to heights unknown.

It would be years later before I truly realized how much ego played a part in many of my decisions and actions. I wanted to win, but would often down-play it or I would remain on the edges until being asked to participate. I would try to keep quiet and draw little attention to myself but that would not last long. There seemed to always be a way of getting in the lime light or a way to advance my agenda.

I am not sure the weightlifting experience was as calculated as some might think, but I am certain it became a catalyst for me stick things out and to not give up. Sometimes it was my ego and pride that kept me engaged, but sometimes it was the possibility of victory. What I have learned is that victory for the sake of victory has a way of weakening one's character and ability to compete and win with integrity.

Lord, give me strength.

Give me strength to hold on to the truths of your word until my change comes.

Give me strength to let go of the things that keep me from growing closer to you and to others.

Give me strength to stretch my spiritual ear and to open my heart so that I can become better acquainted and acclimated to your voice and the direction you have charted for my life.

Lord, give me strength to make it through this day and to experience at least one more victory.

I have seen you at work before and I am utterly impressed. You have taken nothing and made everything. You have taken nobody's and made them kings and rulers of their domain. You have cleaned the hearts of men and women who had been stained by sin and shame. You have redirected the path of those who had chosen their own way to destruction.

I have seen you at work before and I am utterly impressed. You have taken me from a place of hiding to mountaintop experiences that allow me to see how far and how wide your love stretches. You have worked through my conservative and liberal views to temper compassion and tolerance for others. I have seen you at work before and I am utterly impressed. You do all things well. You do all things in abundance. You do all things for your people. You do all things well. Thank you. Amen.

Thoughts On Hanging

I was waiting in line at the Post Office when I overheard a conversation between two women. When they first approached each other the one asked the other, "Girl, how are you doing?" The woman replied, "I'm hanging in there. Doing the best I can with what I can." To which the friend replied, "Good for you!"

Now on one level this was a positive exchange. Maybe the woman had gone through some terrible struggles and was doing the best she possibly could to [simply] still be alive. I suppose it really caught my attention because "hanging" is closely associated with lynching, being strung up or even with standing idle with little or no purpose. Hanging is a passive state. Hanging happens when all hope is lost and or there seems to be no other way to cope.

When one is hanging, s/he can be pushed or pulled in any/many directions by others or by the surrounding elements. If one is hanging, that one has little strength or power to change the situation or to change course without great assistance.

I wonder if those women know the Word of God NEVER tells us to "hang" anywhere. "*Therefore, put on the whole armor of God that you may be able to withstand in the evil day, and, having done all, to stand. Stand therefore...*" (Ephesians 6:13-14a) "*But thanks be to God, who gives us the victory through our Lord Jesus Christ. Therefore, my beloved brothers and sisters, stand firm, be immovable, always abounding in the Lord's work, because you know that your labor is not in vain in the Lord*." (I Corinthians 15:57-58)

We have been given the power to stand firm in every situation. Standing firm allows us to hold our ground while all around us is crumbling and falling apart. Standing firm vs. hanging in keeps us from being pushed around by any/everyone we encounter. You and I can stand upon every promise of God. You and I can stand upon the truth that God will never leave us and God will never forsake us. Finally, hanging is a way of ending one's life; standing is a way of claiming and securing one's space in this life.

So, the next time someone asks, "How are you doing?" You have an option of sending a message of one with dangling feet who can be taken advantage of or be pushed and pulled in many directions. Or you can speak boldly with words that communicate your strength and commitment as a person of faith.

The choice is yours to live and to share as you feel, but if I happen to be in line behind you, I will remind you of the Word of God and the power you have to stand firm upon what you know to be true about God - regardless of what the World may be showing or telling you.

Dear God, give me the strength to stand on your word and to be supported by principles of righteousness and faith. I appreciate you for whom and for what you are in my life. You give me exactly what I need, by way of trials, tests and triumphs so I can see you at work and so I can see my faith grow.

For all the years and for all the opportunities I have allowed to pass without knowing or acknowledging that, thank you. Given where I am right now in my faith development, I trust your word to sustain me in every situation and through every circumstance.

I trust your spirit to guide me in every conversation and through all manner of contemplation. I trust your presence to provide me with confidence in every task and through every valley. Help me, as the hymn begs, "Help me be able to stand. Amen.

Thoughts On Mysterious Ways

You have heard it proclaimed that "God works in mysterious ways, his wonders to perform." But, have you ever read that in the Bible?

Although it is not certain where this truth was first coined, it is obviously true to anyone who has come to realize that God is at work in the world. You know that God has some curious and peculiar ways of reaching the lost, propping up the stumbling, comforting the weak, challenging the strong, and loving all of us – no matter what. God's ways are far above your ways and God's thoughts are far above your thoughts. Even with that you know that God's ways are mysterious and God has a message that will not cease until all that God has set forth has been accomplished.

There are many *sayings* not found in The Bible, but are touted within our common vernacular and quoted frequently by *Saints* and *Aints* in our cities and suburbs and in progressive and conservatives circles.

Each statement deserves a full thought and those may be forthcoming in a future volume, but for now the truth of the matter is that none of those quotations are found in Scripture, but that alone does not negate the affect each one has on one who testifies of their truth and those who bear witness by mere circumstantial means.

For example: We are commanded to praise God in several places in the Bile. We see examples of individuals and communities praising God, with signs following. One distinct way of praising God is through obedience to God's commands. When God instructed Moses to speak words of admonitions to Pharaoh, God honored the commitment to set Moses' people free.

God told Noah what to do in order to save himself and the genesis of the new creation. In response to Noah's obedience, God spared Noah and his family and allowed their sacrifice to be the impetus for the newly populated world.

In Acts 16, Paul and Silas were shackled and chained in a Macedonian jail. Although they were in prison, not sure of their future, they were singing and praising God. In the midst of their prayers and their praise, a great rumbling took place and shook loose their shackles and chains. There are no less than four dozen lessons in that text alone, but for our purpose it is a shining example of praises preceding blessings.

Assigning a truth to a text, based on experience is admirable and expected. However, diluting a text and stripping it of full power is inexcusable and it must cease. The reason this is problematic is because one way we dilute a text is by misquoting it. Assigning a saying biblical 'significance' is different from misquoting a text, but one offense worse than misquoting is 'under-quoting' a text. An example of this is found in Proverbs 4:7: "In all your getting, get understanding (KJV)" People will often say "In all your getting get <u>an</u> understanding." The problem with under-quoting the text here is it lends itself to a limited scope of what the text calls for. The language in the scripture calls for grasping and seeking understanding continuously, not once as the use of "an" suggests. It is a small word, but leaving it out has great consequences.

God, although I sometimes doubt whether I am right or wrong, I never doubt your presence and your ability to lead me to whatever truth or understanding I need for me to move closer to what you desire for me. If unveiling more of will limit the ways in which you move me forward, then remain a mystery because what I do know about you works for me – openly and in secret. And so it is!

Thoughts On This Too Shall Pass

When horrible situations overtake us and we have little hope for moving past them, we often find comfort in hearing or remembering, "This too shall pass." Although that exact phrase is not found in scripture, the truth of that scripture is definitely embedded in many biblical stories and texts, such as:

> *Weeping may endure for the night, but joy comes in the morning (Ps 30:5); Jacob wrestled with an angel of the Lord, the man then said, "Let me go, for it is daybreak." But Jacob said, "I will not let you go until you bless me."* (Gen. 32:27)

The lists of individuals who held on and made it through their trials exceed the bounds of the Holy Bible. You can see living examples in your own circle of influence and in the lives of recent and historic figures. It seems that somehow knowing trouble will not last always not only provides hope, but it is hope.

As you look at your life, today, know that unless you are in heaven, whatever the situation, whatever the trial, whatever the hurdle, whatever the pain, whatever – this too shall pass.

Lord, I am in a situation right now that has my mind and spirit in bondage. I cannot think about anything else, my soul is troubled because of the stress and worry I carry upon my heart. I try not worrying but I find myself worrying about not worrying about my situation. I try not involving others in my stuff, but I feel so alone in this.

Lord, I have to trust you now to lead me from where I am to where you want me to be. I am finding it hard to hold on. I need assurance in my heart and soul that this too shall pass. Amen.

Thoughts On To Thine Own Self Be True

The quote, "To thine own self be true," is taken from Shakespeare's Hamlet, when the character, Polonius, is going about the business of advising the King when he uttered that indelible phrase that has taken on a life of its own.

Polonius was not a biblical character, nor was he a Christian, so he obviously was not aware that it is the Holy Spirit who leads and guides the one who trusts in God. If you put your trust in your own strength, knowledge, and resources then you must be true ONLY to yourself. However, if you trust the Spirit and rely on God's guidance, wisdom and protection, then you must be true to the one who supplies all your needs according to "His riches in glory in Christ Jesus" (Philippians 4:13).

This is not to say that no one is entitled to thoughts or perceptions about one's self that differ from others or what is deemed the norm. Instead, what is proposed for consideration is the fact that God is the author and finisher of our faith and it is God who deserves truth, reverence and loyalty, not one's own ego or physical presence.

This world is full of pleasures and temptations that compete for attention and loyalty, but it is the spirit of God that empowers us to make right choices, even when our desires are in direct competition with what God directs.

So, be true to God and God's word, and in so doing, you will be true to the truth that is in you.

God, help me to be true to you as I follow your lead and trust the plan you have for my life. When I slip into thinking that I have it all figured out, please get me back in line. Amen.

Thoughts On Saying Yes

You may recall the story about the man who was sick for thirty-eight years (John 5). Jesus asked the man, "Do you want to be made well?" the man went on to tell Jesus that every time the angel stirs the water, that someone else gets into the water before he does. Thus, he remains ill and waiting. See, the story that was held true at that time was that at a certain time an angel would come trouble the waters and whoever stepped into the water first would be healed. The man said that he did not have anyone to put him in the pool – he was sick and without assistance, but he had an explanation for why he was sick and without assistance. The writer gives the impression the man and others around him were fully aware of his condition.

Jesus asked, "Do you want to be made well?" After hearing the man's explanation about his lonely condition, Jesus said, "Take up your mat and walk." The man took up his mat and he walked straight into worship. He did not meander about the City. He did as he was commanded to do.

It was in this worship, and I do not mean an 11:00am worship service, but I mean in his walking in obedience to Jesus' words – trusting what he said, he was no longer in his lonely condition. He welcomed the hand and grace of Jesus at the point of desperation and pain, but by faith he received his breakthrough and experienced true deliverance. It took Jesus' words and the man's obedience to his Word to make his impossible dreams into true realities. By accepting Jesus's words, the man acknowledged Jesus' way as an acceptable option. The man did not bargain his way to some middle ground, nor did he ask for an extension because he clearly realized when Jesus extended his hand, he was extending grace beyond measure.

Worship put him in the presence of God and in the presence of others. By moving from where he was to where Jesus called him, he moved beyond what had held him hostage. Unfortunately it was his placement that made him lonely and it was his belief in someone/thing other than God and what God could do that kept him in his condition. We have options before us. We can choose to hear and head Jesus' words or we can listen to ourselves and others. We can choose to worship God in spirit and in truth or we can insist upon hymns and spiritual songs within a 60-minute construct that does little to inspire us beyond the last note. We can bow down and worship at his feet or we can sit on our stools of do-nothing until he returns. We have a choice.

The man at the pool had a choice. He could have heard Jesus' words and went on his way, but he chose to hear the word and to move out into worship. It makes me believe that there is some healing balm found in obedience as an act of worship. It leads me to believe that worship is a natural check-up and preventive step in our redemption and deliverance. We must choose worship and live. We must choose worship and love. We must choose worship and share. We must choose worship and move beyond those places that hold us back and limit our access to life and love.

Are you ready to be made well? Are you whole enough to worship?

God, help me offer the righteous answer to your question. When you ask me if I trust you, help me say "Yes!" When you ask me if I will obey your word, help me say "Yes!" When you ask me if I am ready and willing to let go of my past, which is keeping me from embracing my future, help me say "Yes!" Whenever you ask me anything, God, help me say "Yes!"

Thoughts On Psalm 118

I will not die but live, and will proclaim what the Lord has done. .. The stone the builders rejected has become the capstone; the Lord has done this, and it is marvelous in our eyes. This is the day the Lord has made; let us rejoice and be glad in it. O Lord, save us; O Lord, grant us success. Blessed is he who comes in the name of the Lord. From the house of the Lord we bless you. The Lord is God, and he has made his light shine upon us. With boughs in hand, join in the festal procession up to the horns of the altar. –Psalm 118

Psalm 118 confirms you can live your life and let your life praise God because God is in control and God will ensure that you experience victory. Let go of the thoughts that you do not deserve anything good in your life – God is in your life and God is good. Let go of the thoughts that you do not deserve love in your life – God is in your life and God is love. Let go of the thoughts that you do not deserve grace. It is true, you do not and you never will, but that does not hinder God's abundant supply and distribution.

Be blessed! Rejoice!

Loving and gracious God, allow my life to honor you.

Allow my offerings of service and sacrifices of praise to be pleasing to you. Allow my will and my mind to become one with your will and your mind.

Allow my desires to fade and yours to take center stage – bringing a spotlight on acts of compassion driven by devotion to you, not submission to ego or pride.

May you be pleased with my presence in your world at the dawning of each new day. Amen.

Thoughts On Give My Money Back

I was minding my own business while dining in Denny's when I *managed to overhear* a conversation taking place at a nearby table. There was an older, rugged looking gentleman seated at a booth. As a tall, slender, well-dressed man passed the booth the rugged man asked, "Can you give me some money to get something to eat?" The tall man replied, Sure. How much do you need?? He replied, "Just a few dollars - just enough for some food."

The two men engaged in idle dialogue for a few minutes and the man eventually passed some money to the other man. I heard words of thanksgiving being shared. However, as the waitress passed their table the tall man stopped the waitress and asked for a menu. He said, "My friend here needs a menu so he can order? The rugged man said, "Naw! I don't want to order. I'm gonna take this money to the grocery store and get some food. The tall man said, "Why would you do that? There is food here." The rugged man responded, "I'm gonna go to the grocery store?" The tall man, very sternly stated, "I know one thing; you gone eat in this restaurant right now, or you gonna give my money back."

The rugged man ordered a Creole Skillet, passed the money to the waitress and thanked the tall man for helping out. The tall man left the restaurant.

God help me to be a cheerful giver when I have gifts to share.

Help me to be a grateful and gracious recipient when gifts are offered or presented to me. Just as I receive your love and grace, I want to freely extend it to others without pause or conditions. Amen.

Thoughts On The Tatted Grandma

It was one of those days when it seemed everyone in the City needed something at this particular retail store. There were only four lanes open, so tempers were flaring, random assessments of the level of customer service were being shared, and strangers were making small talk about how much they hated waiting. As usual, I was minding my own business when I noticed the family in front of me. There was a woman who was clearly in her sixties with three teenage girls. The elder woman told the older of the teenagers to stop "smarting off."

When the teenager did not adhere to the request, the elder woman stepped very quickly and sternly into close proximity of the girl. She said something about knocking her into the middle of next week and several other things that let me and other onlookers know who was in charge. As the woman stepped toward the girl, I saw a very large tattoo on her arm that read "I’m not the one" with a picture of a teddy bear below it. The girl said, "Dang grandma!"

Grandma was not one with whom I or anyone who feared for their life would challenge. Every few seconds after that, grandma issued an admonition to the teenager. Somehow the teenagers were able to tune her out in a way that I was not.

While we were waiting there another woman approached me from behind and asked if she and her four little ones could go ahead of me since they only had one item. I acquiesce and said "Good luck getting past the next crew." she said, "Whew! I'm scared to ask them." she waited a few minutes, and then she asked grandma if she could go ahead of her with her little ones and their one item.

Without looking directly at the woman, grandma said, "I been in this line for the longest. Why you gonna ask me that?" Grandma snarled a little more before giving permission. My thoughts of judgment and ridicule were in high-gear and in hot pursuit at that point. Did she always function at such a high level of anxiety? Was it necessary for her to terrorize her granddaughters and strangers? I was also wondering what would happen to me if she knew I was running those questions through my mind?

As grandmas moved beyond a very large column that had been blocking her view of the cashier and the conveyer belt, the cashier said, "Oh my God! I haven't seen you in years. I'm Tracy." Grandma put on a huge smile and let out a laugh as she responded with joy and amazement. Grandma became so enthralled in the exchange with the cashier and really became a different person instantly. I could see a loving, nurturing side of the seemingly hard, harsh, rough talking, tattooed woman who moments earlier had frightened me and others with her stance and with her words. I judged her as a burly woman with little good to offer those teenage girls. I wondered about their care and self-worth. I thought about my own grandmother and other older women who carried themselves with more regal tones of speech and would never, ever have a tattoo on their 14" forearms.

As I moved in closer I could hear enough of the conversation to gather that the cashier had been a childhood friend of grandmother's daughter. Grandma pointed toward two of the teenagers as she said, "I bet you don't know who that is." The cashier said, "No! It can't be." grandma said, "Yes! Don't they look just like their mama?" Tracy replied, "Oh my God! I remember when they were born," looking at the girls, "you were little girls last time I saw y'all." Grandma said, "I've raised them since their mother got killed." Suddenly the story came together.

The cashier was childhood friends with two of the girl's mother and that was how she knew grandma. My heart went out to those girls and to grandma because I could only imagine the pain and anguish that would come as the result of losing a mother and daughter. Could that be why grandma was so angry and stern with those girls? Had she been that way with her own daughter? Regardless of the answers to the many questions in my head, I felt I had judged this woman too quickly and too harshly, given this new revelation.

Grandma asked Tracy for a pen and paper to write her phone number on it. As grandma wrote the number she looked up and asked Tracy, "What y'all used to call me, Miss Joyce?" She said, "Yes ma'am. I will give this to my mom so she can call you...She will be glad to talk to you after all these years." As grandma and the girls began to roll their two carts away, grandma yelled back to Tracy, "I'm putting in an application for here so it's good to know you work here and you can give me a good reference." Tracy said, "Bye Miss Joyce."

I placed my items on the belt and paid for my items as I reflected on what had just happened within my own heart and mind while observing and judging that woman because of her 'appearance.' I felt bad about my thoughts and actions. I had judged her very harshly without knowing anything about her story or her struggle. I did not know if she has been abused by her husband or other men. I did not know if other women had taken advantage of her and contributed to her feeling as though she was alone in this world. I did not know if she had been wrongfully accused and convicted for a crime, without adequate alibi or representation. I climb high atop my judgment seat and cast so much judgment on her without giving it much thought. I felt so bad for what I had done until I exited the store and heard a familiar voice at full volume with hands on her hips, "Naw! We do not have time for you to get McDonald's! Y'all know I have to go to school. Let's go!"

Yes! It was grandma.

Lord, you created this world and everything in it- the Earth, the moon, the stars and that inhabits the Earth. Everything was created by you. You even created the noise and volume we need to cry out when necessary. But, you did not stop there.

You created ways for us to escape danger of all kinds. You even created places of shelter and shalom where you reside and can begin to heal us. Thank you for that.

God, I am reminded that you created the ones who sin as well as the ones who sin against us. I struggle with thanking you for the sinner, but given I am one of them I ask for forgiveness and strength to continue to forgive myself and those who sin against me.

God, as I reflect on the actions of the grandmother and my perceptions about her, I ask your forgiveness for passing judgment on her and her grandchildren.

I could add, I did not know their stories, but that is irrelevant. Their stories or the paths taken to get to that point in life and in that line were of little value and it should be of little consequence when I have the power to choose between praying and judging.

Again, God, forgive me.

Thank you and help me to shun opportunities to abuse anyone or anything within your creation. Amen.

Thoughts On Folklore About Coffee

Any time I venture into a coffee shop, I notice there are more and more teens and even children in line placing orders just as complicated as the adult's orders.

On one hand it causes me concern because they know so much about coffee drinks. I am still now sure of the difference between an espresso, latte or cappuccino. But they seem to know and they express their orders with glee. Seeing so many young people at coffee houses also causes me concern because when I was young, my grandmother told us "drinking coffee will make you blacker" and someone else said, "drinking coffee will put hair on your chest."

If any of that is true, then we are going to have a generation or more of little girls getting darker and growing chest hair. Seriously, how many other cultural truisms or folklore still linger with us and impact our ability to engage the world or others? Has anyone's finger ever fallen off after pointing to a graveyard? What about splitting poles or stepping on cracks?

We do not know where those phrases or superstitions originated, but we know how they are perpetuated from generation-to-generation. That is why it is important to examine the source of our knowledge and faith. We must know the origins so we can speak with confidence and pass along good and helpful knowledge to those who will live beyond our years.

God, you are the one who laughs when we laugh, you cry when we cry and you mourn when we mourn. You give us liberty through your spirit to explore ourselves and your world. Thank you for freedom to choose you. Thank you for freedom to choose to love. Amen.

Thoughts On Not Knowing What You Have

In some airports the security lines are marked for 'Expert' travelers and 'Crew' vs. lines for 'Family' and 'Casual' travelers. I usually choose the Expert line because the business travelers and those who fly more than they drive tend to occupy that line. It moves very efficiently when the right people get in that line. But, when the wrong person slips in, it is total mayhem.

I had not experienced such mayhem until that one fateful day when a woman wearing one of those blue Hillary Clinton pant suits got in front of me in the Expert line. She looked the part, so I had no reason to question her ability or willingness to get through the checkpoint as quickly as possible.

We approached the conveyor belt and she removed her laptop, her keys, belt and shoes. As I followed her lead I heard a commotion at the scanner, "Bag check!" I looked around as if that voice was coming from one of the other stations. The woman looked back at me as if I was the cause of the problem. As if!

The attendants rushed over to the scanner and retrieved her neat little briefcase and pulled bottle of water from her bag. She looked around, confused and said, "I had no idea what was in there."

I would have been upset with the woman for messing up our blue streak through security, except her calamity was the impetus for me thinking about how many times I have done something, later to realize the Bible has something to say about the situation.

God, your word shall be engrafted upon my heart and flow from lips, so that I will know the power of your Word in every situation. I want to know and to live what is in there. Amen.

Thoughts On A New Perspective

If you have ever spent any time in Los Angeles, you know that you never see stars in the sky. One familiar and constant view above the city at night is the lights from the incoming planes.

While serving as a Youth Pastor in Compton, I was visiting with one of the church families and the older of the boys walked me to my car after the visit. We looked up into the sky and saw a long line of lights from incoming planes.

As we gazed into distant sky, he laughed. I asked, "What's funny?" He said, "When we were little we went to visit my aunt in Arizona. One night when we were sitting out in her backyard, my little brother said, 'I wonder where all of those planes are going.' We all laughed and told him those were not planes; those are stars."

It takes getting out of our familiar surroundings to see things differently and to experience common things in new ways. For those boys, the sky had only been a place for planes and lights, but in a new environment, they learned the sky is full of stars at night. Those same stars are in Los Angeles, but they are hidden by all of the pollution.

The same is true for us. The good we need to experience in life is sometimes clouded or blocked by pollution that we cannot control or may not realize is there. Pollution in our lives can be unhealthy habits, over-extended relationships, or unrealistic expectations of us and others. But, when we are able to step back and take a look from a different angle, we can see things for what they are really made of.

Creator and sustainer of all life, continue to hold my hand as I walk the paths you have destined for me to walk. Amen.

Thoughts On Meeting Famous People

While in Washington, D.C. for the Martin Luther King, Jr. Memorial Dedication, I was standing near the valet stand of the host hotel. A little white Honda Accord (or similar model) pulled up to the valet stand. The door opened and out stepped Cheryl Underwood in a very nice white, evening gown. I greeted her and she began talking about how good all the men standing around there was looking. While she was checking us out, I asked a Brother standing near me: "Why are they driving her around in that car?"

On my flight back to Los Angeles, I had a brief layover in Nashville. Prior to boarding the plane I was notified that I had been granted a First Class upgrade. Yay!

I boarded the plan and took my seat in the fourth row window seat. A young woman was already seated in the third row window seat when I boarded the plane. I saw her, but did not pay her very much attention. As people started filing onto the plane I noticed several of them looking at the woman in the third row. I became curious, as I wanted to know who they were admiring up there. I could only see that she had red hair and she was overly engrossed in her IPhone activities. Finally someone sat in the seat next to me and I asked: "Do you know who this woman is in front of us?" He replied, "I am not from this country, but I assume it is one of your big stars."

The first famous person I met was Quincy Jones. The most impressive famous person I ever met was Ruby Dee and with all stars, they are just people. Some of them are living their dreams, while others are living a nightmare.

God, thank you for blessing me to be me. Amen.

Thoughts On Parenting a Parent

A man was driving next to me on Manchester Boulevard. As we approached the intersection at Prairie Avenue, I overheard him on the phone. He was speaking with his mother's landlord.

He said, "I am calling on behalf of my mother. She has been having some trouble with getting her rent and stuff together. I am on my way to you right now with $400.00. [And] I want to know if I can bring the other $350.00, in a week or two." There was a pause. The he said, "Yes! I am on my way right now."

I had thoughts of judgment and wonder: What kind of life had his mother lived that she was not able to pay her rent in full? What kind of son was he that he could not pay his mother's rent? Why was he driving a nearly new German sedan, if he was not in a position to assist his mother financially, if needed? What happens if the landlord refuses the partial payment? Is the son in position to receive his mother into his home? What if he currently lives with his mother?

The occurrence I happen to overhear gets played out every day in many ways. In every case where a child must tend to the affairs of their parent, there is great sacrifice involved.

We see this with adult children learning to care for a parent with Alzheimer's, dementia, aging, while also struggling with a generation behind them who are not financially or emotionally stable enough to care for themselves. There are issues of underemployment, excessive education, incarceration, debt and rising housing costs. The adult child with adult children and aging parents are participants in what is known as the "Sandwich generation" – they are firmly placed between a parent and a child who need them equally.

Lord, have mercy! Grant caregivers patience and peace. Amen.

Thoughts On In-Flight Security

Over the years I have flown on many airplanes with many airlines and far too many flight crews to count. The seating choice, comfort of the seat, taste of the food (back when it was served), selection of beverages, and temperature all vary from flight-to-flight. But there is one consistent element on every flight – the safety briefing.

Whether it is offered in English and Spanish or German and Korean, the message is the same: "Place your oxygen mask on first before assisting other passengers."

We are reminded of the need to secure ourselves first. That is not the scenario for heroes or *sheroes* to emerge from the crowd because if for some reason you are without adequate oxygen for a prolonged period of time, you could suffer brain injuries. You could be left without proper motor skills to assist yourself later. You could die. You are in a far-better position and condition to help others, if you take care of yourself first.

This is also true when you are going about your normal work or activities. You must care for your spiritual, physical and emotional self so that you can be healthy enough to share with others. When we care for ourselves we fill our tanks and we are able to share the overflow with others. We are able to exude confidence and care from a full reservoir of compassion and concern; instead of a place of depleted energy and a defeatist attitude.

You are an awesome God. You take us high and bring us low – staying with us in every phase of our journey.

Thank you for energy and intellect to move through each day. May my reports of good health continue. Amen.

Thoughts On "I Am"

Michael Beckwith, founder and spiritual director of Agape International Spiritual Center said, "When you know who you are, you are less interested and less motivated by what others can do for you or to you because you are aware of your strength and greatness because of who and what resides within you."

On those Sundays when I am not tasked to be in attendance at a United Methodist Church or a conference, I attend Agape. I was first introduced to the live and in person experience of Agape a few years ago when a friend invited me to attend. He had heard Beckwith on Oprah and had become intrigued by his message. Although I had heard of Agape and Beckwith, I had never been tempted to attend services or to read any of his books. However, after only 10-minutes into that first worship experience, I was a believer in the message and the method.

As I looked around that worship center, I saw people of every nation and tongue, every age and socio-economic group was standing to their feet, joining together in song. There was exuberance in the air and in the exchange taking place in the worship space.

It was in the midst of that dynamic message that Beckwith began to talk about how important it is for us to know who we are in relation to the divine, spiritual nature within us – not in relation to our biological counterparts, but our spiritual reality. I had never heard anything like that in any church I had attended. Suddenly the divine had my full attention.

Before he closed out the message and had us turn and prophesy to our neighbors about ourselves, he said: "When you know who you are, you are less interested and less motivated by what others can do for you or to you because you are aware of your strength and greatness because of who and what resides within you."

When he said it, I knew it was something I needed to record, reflect upon and begin seeking right away. I had to get to a place where I was sure of my identity and my character, apart from my vocation, but core to my call to be a spiritual being in this world. I had to get beyond what others thought and get in touch with what the Divine thinks of and through me. I left that day sure I would return for more...and I have.

God, help me accept the love you give to me. Allow me presence of mind to know that you are at work, working things out for my good – regardless of how it looks or feels.

I want to get to that place in life where I truly walk by faith and not by sight. I want to get to that place in life where I truly believe that greater is he that is in me than he that is in the world. I want to get to that place where I truly believe that I am more than a conqueror through him who loves me.

I want to get to that place where I truly believe that though I walk through the valley of the shadow of death that I fear no evil and I know that God is with me.

I want to get to that place where I truly believe that the battle is not mine, it's the Lord's. I want to get to that place where I truly believe that weeping may endure for the night but joy comes in the morning. I want to get to that place where I truly believe that if I call, God will answer.

I want to know who I am the way the Divine experiences me in the world. I want to be more than what I perceive I am or can be. I want to be motivated by the divine order of the universe instead of begin wooed by the whims of the world or the latest gimmick of the church.

Well, God, this is my call. I shall await your response.

Thoughts On A Dog In A Carrier

That mini pinscher was scrunched down in that faux Louis Vuitton carrier, as if he was made for it and it was made for him. As I caught the pup's wondering eye, my thoughts raced to a place where I questioned how often I had been in an uncomfortable situation or predicament, but appeared to be fine with it. Had I done such a good job fooling others that I was also convinced of my own unfamiliar truth? If so, how had that created rifts in my relationship with God and others?

God, help me love you more today.

I want to reach out to you. I want and need you to reach up, over and beyond all of the barriers I have set that keep me away from you. Pull me, push me, lift me and do whatever you have to do to get me closer to you.

I have struggled to let go of enough of my pride and ego to share this with you. Even though I know that you know all there is to know about me. Even though I know that you know everything I will say and do in advance. Even though I know that you are committed to working things out for my good. Even though I have seen you at every turn and I have heard you call to me before I reached my dead ends. Even though I see you and hear you at work on my life, I still try to block myself from you.

It's funny I want the blessings, but I find myself avoiding the source of all blessings. I want and need to stop doing that. As I think about it I realize that if the blessings are this good with all of ME in the way, I can only imagine what it will be when you get me out of the way.

So, do what you have to do to get to me and to get through to me.
I want you to do this for me, so I can do more for you.
This is my prayer, today. Amen.

Thoughts On Thoughts About Myself

You must talk to yourself about yourself and you must talk about yourself to yourself if you are ever going to gain a great appreciation for who you are. You must recalibrate your thoughts. If you are to successfully recalibrate your thoughts you must pay close attention to what you say and believe about your humanity and your divinity. You must be vigilant about what you allow to seep out of your mouth and into your heart. Prayer and devotional disciplines work wonders in the retooling process. Pay attention to what you pray about yourself and what you believe about prayer as you pray the following prayer:

God, transform me from a spirit of 'me' to a spirit of 'you.' Help me let go of what I want and begin to praise you and thank you for what you provide. I know I come to you most often as if I am approaching Santa Claus. I tell you what I want and expect you to deliver it just because it is what I want.

I come to you as if you are a genie. I rub my hands together and expect you grant my wishes, just so you can stay in my good graces. I sometimes come to you as if you are a secretary, by dictating what I want and you are to figure out how to get it to me by the deadline I set or that is implied in the tone of my voice.

I expect you to know my thoughts before I think them. I expect you to know my words before I speak them. I expect you to read my mind. Unfortunately you do read my mind, you do hear my words, and you do see everything I do. But, fortunately, because of your grace, you see my heart and its truest intent.

I want to get out of myself and get more into you. Allowing you to receive me as is and to prepare me and present me as you desire. Help me offer myself and my words as sacrifices to you all day, each day. When I am able to allow you to work in this way, then my spirit will point toward 'you.' Amen.

Thoughts On Minor Agreements

Minor agreements often have major unintended consequences because the effects are cumulative and feed our habits and urges, which work contrary to the flowing of the spirit in our lives.

Minor agreements are those little excuses we make for ourselves – those little habits and activities that are often hidden, but have a way of piling up and coming into view at some point.

As followers of Christ, we are to deal honestly and justly with others and with ourselves. Doing harm to any portion of God's creation is sin that must be acknowledged and overcome.
It is easy to make minor agreements to "stop before it goes too far" or "gets in the way of our relationships." But we often are unaware that things have gone too far and our relationships have hit the skids long before we realize how bad things have gotten.
Lying, cheating, deceiving and misleading ourselves and others are on the short list of minor agreements we make that have major consequences.

Lord, I have great difficulty managing my own affairs. Please grant me the wisdom I need to discern what is my business and what is your business.

When I discover it's mine, I pray that I rely on you to get me through it.

When I discern it's not my business, I pray that I can be faithful enough to trust you to continue to work in that person's life and situation the way you see fit.

This is new for me, but I need to mind my own business and come clean on where I am in my relationships and in my secret dealings. Give me grace to focus on those things. That should keep me busy for a while. So help me God. Amen.

Thoughts On Paying Attention

During the 2011, Annual Conference Session, the attendees were voting for General Conference delegates. There were several things going on with one piece of legislation that was before the body. People were making motions to amend the item, delete sections of the item and some even wanted to table it for a later time. I was so confused by what was happening. I heard the Bishop say, "Let's move on to another item of business." That is when I asked a colleague "Did we vote or act on the previous item?" She said, "No! We did not. Go to the microphone and let her know before we move on."

I ran over to the microphone to be recognized to speak. The Bishop acknowledged me and I asked if we were going to take action on the previous item. Bishop responded, "We did take action, what were you doing?" I said, "Sorry Bishop, but Catie was talking to me." The auditorium erupted in laughter.

That incident was hilarious on its own merit, but it was the Bishop's follow-on that took it to a higher level. After everyone quieted down, she said, "After casting your previous ballot, you have elected Cedrick Bridgeforth as a delegate to General Conference." After a brief applause, she continued, "Maybe Catie should tell him he was elected, so he won't miss that information." Again, laughter filled the auditorium and for all the right reasons.

How often has being right and doing right become so tantamount in the moment that simply being in the moment has not entered the picture?

God, I trust you to lead us in ways that challenge our thinking and expand our beliefs and faith in you. So, I ask you to help us to be more confident in you than we are in our own intellect and insights. I trust you to forgive us and sharpen our spiritual ear that we may hear you clearer. Amen.

Thoughts On Unsuspecting Grooms

It was a hot August evening as I walking along with a dear friend from our hotel to a formal engagement at another venue. Although the heat index dictated otherwise, we opted to walk instead of taking a taxi. Ordinarily this would not have been a great concern but we were both wearing tuxedos, mine with tails, in the DuPont Circle neighborhood of Washington, D.C.

As we were walking toward an intersection, there was a woman walking toward us carrying several bags. We noticed her as she placed the bags behind a planter and began approaching us. As she came near us she said, "The flowers are so beautiful and you are going to be so happy. Oh! Yes! Your wedding is going to be so special!"

I looked at him and he looked at me. We fell over laughing. One source of humor was that she assumed we were en route to a wedding – our wedding. The second source was that we were actually going to a Martin Luther King, Jr. Memorial Dedication event.

Context for sharing one's truth is important. The woman saw two men in an area of a City where same-gender marriage is not illegal and she made an assumption, based on the context, that we were not only going to a wedding but we were going to our wedding. We saw the woman walking with several bags and made an assumption, based on the context, she was homeless and probably not mentally stable.

I am certain we were not walking to our wedding, but there was little time for us to engage the woman in a way to share the truth of the matter with her. All we know is that she was happy and happy for us. Maybe that was exactly what she needed in that moment. We laughed then and continue to laugh as we think about it.

After the encounter with the woman our conversation shifted from mundane rants about the heat to a solemn recognition that we were in a context where the political realities were different where we were walking than they are where we live and work. The woman was free to speak her truth. Men and women all around us were free to marry as they chose.

We were going to an event celebrating a man who protested and died so that all people would be treated equal in the United States of America and beyond. Perhaps her contextual mishap was exactly what we needed to take our minds off the heat and the walk, while helping us focus on the varying degrees of freedom shared and limited all around us.

Lord, help us share our truth as we know it and in ways that bring joy, not sorrow to others. When we get it wrong, forgive us and help us gain a new and better perspective that will empower all to continue living and sharing as you desire.

In moments when we are judgmental and careless with others, forgive us. In situations where we assume the role of bigot and treat others as though they were created by someone other than you, forgive us. In moments when we victimize others for who you have created them to be, forgive us. In situations where we minimize the contributions of others for what you have called them to do, forgive us. In moments when we fail to see that when we revel in our own success, others may be victimized for lack of that same victory, forgive us.

Please open our hearts to your will and your way in the world. Open our eyes to see the good that is around us. Open our heart to feel the pain of others. Open our territory to walk the way of those with less [obvious] privilege or ego.

May your world be made whole as a result of our commitment to look for ways to love and to serve you and your people more faithfully. All this we ask in the name of you, our Creator. Amen.

Thoughts On Intercession

After a few hours in an airport during major delay periods can be nerve-racking. Add to the uncomfortable seats, unpleasant gate agents a few mile-long lines at the food counters and you have the makings of a summer blockbuster disaster movie.

While waiting in one of those lines, there was a man with his two young sons in line ahead of me. I had watched the dad struggle with the boys to keep them near him and close together for quite a while. As we got closer to the front of the line, he said to the eldest of the boys: "Go ask mom what she wants?" The boys scurried off to the waiting area and ran back to dad as fast as they could. The younger of the boys replied, "She said, get her a soy latte and a little...hmmm...something and a bottle of water." Dad replied, "Thanks buddy! That was real helpful."

There are times when intermediaries are not useful, while at other times they are necessary, practical or the only way to move things along. For instance, in prayer, we have intercessors – those who speak on our behalf for things and in situations known and unknown to us. Intercessors may not have the full story of our dealings but they do have full access to the one who can heal, save, forgive and restore. One who intercedes for others in prayer is an intermediary who does not need the full story.

The intercessor only needs to be willing to access the one who does know the past, present and future. By accepting that one can only pray when one knows the full story is disastrous. The little boys were doing what they could, given their capacity. It may not have been all that the father needed, but it got him focused in the right direction. I tapped him on the shoulder and told him I would hold his place while he went to get his wife's full order.

God, I surrender my prayer time to your agenda and to the agenda of others. I avail myself to speak on behalf of others as your spirit guides me. Amen.

Thoughts On Privacy

While sitting in the waiting area in an airport, I overheard a man on the phone, shouting: "I am calling to find out if there is a problem with my account or with my ATM card because it was declined last night...My Social is 524*3*8537...Yes, my date of birth "twelve, nineteen, forty-seven...I am not sure what address you have for my last known address, but try 8642 Silverado Lane. Oh! Wait! I found my account number and my security code. Do you want me to give it to you?" At that point the gate agent made a very loud announcement, so I missed the next couple exchanges between the man and the bank rep.

After the gate agent announcement ended, I overheard the man say: "It is amazing. Due to privacy concerns and theft issues, I never carry or write checks so I don't ever have my account number in front of me. But it's here in my IPad® with all my other numbers my son put on here for me...The number is 388243****9753."

I was sitting there in absolute amazement at what I had overheard in a wide-open public space. However, as we go through life, sometimes we give away what we would never want others to have, then we wonder how that happened. That is true in regard to identity theft, cyber-crimes and crimes of the heart. We expose ourselves to others, making ourselves completely vulnerable and fail to realize the damage that can be done to us.

Not everyone who receives your information will use it to harm you. Some will use it to help you improve how you see and how you may protect yourself in the future.

All wise God, grant me a spirit of discernment so that I may know who and what is in my life to strengthen me. Help me to hold fast to those relationships and situations that improve my situation. Give me courage to release those that will do me harm and help me to not miss their presence. Amen.

Thoughts On People Staring

I was walking into Wal-Mart as I overheard one guy say to another, "I hate it when people just be staring at you, but scared to open their mouth and say something." The other guy responded, "Who are you talking about?" He replied, "That dude I was looking at over there. He just kept staring."

Of course my mind kicked into high-gear. How would this guy have known the other guy was staring at him unless he was staring back at him?

Sometimes we have to pause and ask ourselves: What am I doing that is causing this situation? What is my part in this ongoing drama? Am I the star, co-star, or the writer/director of this reality? In the case of the staring incident, there was only one way for this to have played out the way it did. The one complaining was clearly a participant in the exchange. He was the star in that he was the object of someone else's attention. He was the co-star in that he was a full participant. He noticed the guy staring at him and instead of walking away, ignoring what he perceived to be the case; he kept looking back at the guy. In some ways he also assumed the role of writer/director because the scene played out as he envisioned it in his heart and mind -- A true renaissance man.

Creator God, you made the world and all that is within and beyond it. You made each of us in your image and in your likeness. We are told that after creating everything, you looked upon it and deemed it "good."

As a being created by you, I am good. Good enough to look upon your creation and behold its beauty. At times my inner and outer appearance seems ugly or distorted. I need you to help me see the beauty you see. Help me hold fast to the good you have imparted to me. Let me play my role in creation. Amen.

Thoughts On Right Living

Someone very close to me received a grave diagnosis from her oncologist. This was the type of news that would shake a woman in her early sixties with 3 adult children, but just imagine what it could do to the average, young, unwed mother of a five year-old. Most would begin taking inventory of their lives, asking tough theological questions, making ontological and mythological connections and assumptions to bring some sense of reason within an incomprehensible reality.

Most would form or begin examining their age-old bucket list(s) or take up a cause to fight what was an inevitable demise. Most would re-examine missteps and missed opportunities - take advantage of options that seemed far-fetched or had been taken for granted. Most would sense the keen twinge in their nostrils as they whiff lavender, oleander, or fresh mint. Suddenly there was keen awareness of the aromatic chasm between oregano and basil.

Some would name and blame every friend, foe, lover and God who had never dared to return love and affection in ways that would make up for lost sleep and tears. Some would envy parents and become enraged by the lavish life choices of siblings and neighbors. Some would chart an ideal course and dance with destruction. Others would determine to fight until the bitter end and refuse to take "No!" for an answer. Not this young woman.

Her responses revealed and called upon a wisdom and faith that betrayed her mere 32 years of experience on earth. She was resolved to use this bad news to make her better. She determined to hear the voice of God that assured her she was healed. She could have joy "unspeakable and full of glory" not for herself, but glory for/to God.

She committed her prayers, as she had since high school, to focus on the needs and ills of others. She knew she had a problem, but she believed God's word: *By [His] stripes [she is] healed and He "came so [she] could experience abundant life"* (John 10:10).

She was not walking around as one who was so heavenly minded that she was no earthly good, but she remained steadfast, unmovable, abounding in the work of the Lord (I Corinthians 15:57-58) - not in response to this bad news the doctors had reported, but in response to the good news she had received from Jesus throughout her life. She did not alter her life to accommodate ill-gained spiritual disciplines or human contrived events to get closer to God. She did not pray longer, join a Bible Study or support group to cope or to manage what she was now facing.

Often when tragedy strikes we have to get things in order or go find the many pieces of our lives to reconnect with what is important or we must further separate from what has seemingly caused us great grief. We prioritize spending less time on less meaningful attitudes and relationships. We struggle to redirect assets and thoughts to plans that do more to impact our landscape less to contact landmarks. The mist of distant waterfalls and vivid colored rainbows remind us of our baptism. Breaking bread with friends becomes holy moments whenever it happens. We realize "if we stay ready, we do not have to get ready!"

The young woman mentioned here had learned to live a faithful life, devoted to living open and free before God. Therefore, when she was dealt what most or some would view as a death sentence, she remained calm, steady and faithful. She sought to stay right (not get right) with God. She was strong in life and expected God's grace and love to grant her what she needed as much in this life as in the next. Righteousness was her goal.

One of the sage professors at Samford University, taught us through deed, not rhetoric, "It is such a small thing to be right." Often what we do and think in hard times and when we desperately seek to overtake the spiritual forces at work in our lives, that somehow we can do the right things or prove ourselves right to avert the projected outcome when being right gets us nowhere. We learn through Scripture and through the testimony of the young woman that faithfulness in discipline and discipleship develops *paths of righteousness* and those paths keep us *near still waters* and merely cast *shadows of death* (Psalm 23).

Most Holy Lord, I trust your word and your will to be sufficient in purpose and power.

I trust you will give me the strength I need to be a disciplined disciple who will follow your lead each day.

I trust you to shepherd me through rough and crooked places.

I trust you to lead me through dark valleys and through plains filled with light. So often you have projected me toward mountain peaks and you have protected me during rapid descent.

I trust you to help me hear bad news through the filter of Good News found in your Word, in my life and in the testimonies of others. So that I may be encouraged to trust you more than ever and I will be able to share of how good you are to me.

My testimony will speak of your compassion and your grace. My testimony will inspire others to reach higher and stand longer than they would have before they learned of what you will do with just a little faith.

My testimony will have all the right words because they will all center on you and what you are doing in my life and in the lives of those around me.

Please, Dear God, continue to be present with me right now as I focus less on doing right things and being right and more on living a righteous life. Amen.

Thoughts On The Rental Car Return

Since it was raining, I arrived at the rental car return exactly 2 hours in advance of my flight. As I exited the car, I noticed there were not any attendants nearby or in sight. I removed my luggage from the trunk, jotted down the mileage, retrieved my copy of the rental contract and proceeded inside to the counter.

Once inside, I had to wait in line behind three angry customers. It was apparent each of them had major issues and their dissatisfaction would impact my ability to make my scheduled flight. I stood there looking as patient and as pleasant as possible – hoping someone would see and believe my case was simple and would be delightful to handle.

The first customer approached with a broken GPS. She explained to the man behind the counter that the GPS could not be working because it would not get her to her intended destination. He asked her, "Ma'am, did you input the correct address?" His question sent my mind on practical and theological journeys. My thoughts centered on how often we think about a destination or we "intend to do" something or go somewhere, but we do not take the necessary steps to actualize any plans that will move us from where we are. Yet, we live with an expectation of getting to that destination. The GPS will only work if you program it and follow it as best you can. Of course we know when we get off course, the GPS is programmed to "recalculate."

The lady was appalled that she was being asked such menial questions by the attendant. Then, as he turned the GPS on, he asked her, "Ma'am, what was the address you were trying to reach?" She muttered an address. He scrolled through the GPS several times and finally he said, "Ma'am, the address you shared with me was never entered in the device. Did you try a different address?" She said, "No! When that stupid thing would not take me where I wanted to go, I shut it off and left it in the console. So, give me a refund for that thing." The attendant said, "Ma'am, I cannot refund you for equipment that is in good condition and will work if used properly." She demanded to speak with his supervisor.

As the second customer approached, he had issues with the amount he was being charged. The attendant asked to see the receipt he was holding. The customer gave him the receipt. The attendant said, "Sir, you initialed in all six places, noting your acceptance of the charges and coverage being offered to you." The customer responded, "I was not aware it would add up to this much, so I should not have to pay that amount." At this point, I expected an even longer delay since this man was steaming mad and he wanted some relief. However, the attendant was firm and direct as he stated the company's policy on coverage and charges. The man eventually grew so angry he grabbed his contract and stormed out the door. He moved so quickly the woman with the GPS was also walking out, and was almost run over by him.

The third customer approached the counter and made apology for the two who had just left. I was upset because she used my Mr. Nice Guy approach I had purposed to use. Her issue was simple, or so it seemed. Her credit card had been charged twice for the same car and amount. She was requesting a refund. The attendant called the manager over and explained the situation. The manager apologized to her and said, "We will get this taken care of right away and you will see the refund to your card in 7-to-10 business days." That is when this nice lady grew horns and pulled out her pitchfork. "Seven days? I only had the car for two days. You [] up my charges and I get penalized for more than a week, why?" I forget what the manager said, but this woman ended up storming out of the lobby much like the two before her.

As I approached, my demeanor was calm and collected because now I have endured over 30-minutes in this lobby and I need to get to the terminal, check my bags and board my flight very soon. The attendant apologized for making me wait and asked, "How may I help you, sir?" I said, "I am returning my vehicle. Here are the keys, the contract and the ending mileage. That should be all you need, so I can be on my way." He smiled and said, "It's never that easy, sir." At that point I began to worry and I wondered if this rental agency had a company policy that insisted the customer was not a priority and must leave the office upset every time. That was a true concern of mine, given the three customers who had gone before me.

He pulled up my account, verified the charges were correct, and gave me a discount off my next rental. He told me the discount coupon was for me being so patient and for "doing what I was supposed to do." To keep matters simple, I expressed gratitude, grabbed my bags from the corner and proceeded to the shuttle. As I boarded the shuttle there was a great verbal fervor in the air. I looked around and all three of the customers who had stormed out were on the shuttle. When I stepped onto the bus, they all turned and looked at me – expecting me to join in the battle. I said, "Let's get this party started!" They laughed and assumed the normal posture of strangers on a bus.

Almighty God, you are in every place working on our behalf. Thank you for caring enough to teach us how to be in relationship with others, with you, and with ourselves.

Often times we miss out on the lessons you want us to learn. We miss out on relationships that can ease our way in the world. We cling to relationships that lessen our impact. We seek companions and opportunities to be exploited and to be explosive, because it is all we know. We set internal policies and tests that make it impossible for those who mean us all the good in the world to access or to penetrate. We find ourselves off course and without recourse for the mistakes we have made. Yet, that is where you work best.

You work best in those places where we have hid ourselves and deplete our resources. You work for our good, even when we decide to rebel instead of rejoicing. Thank you, Almighty God.

Thoughts On Uncertain Future

In DFW Airport, 4 young men boarded the tram singing a song from my distant past "off we go into the wild blue yonder, flying high...nothing can stop the U S Air Force!" they were full of vigor and energy. The four of them were not familiar with each other, yet. I knew they would become utterly intimate with each other and be grateful for their camaraderie in just a few short hours.
It was September 21, 1988, when I boarded a bus at the Air Force recruitment office in Decatur, Alabama. My mom dropped me off that morning. All I had with me where the clothes I was wearing, a change of clothes in my recently purchased trumpet case, which doubled as my suitcase and an old rugged, pocket-sized King James Version of the Bible. As I boarded the bus my mom gave me a handwritten note. I waved good-bye to her and my recruiter and began to shed tears of uncertainty.

I was 18 years old and had made the decision almost a year earlier to enlist in the Air Force. Some people have asked why and if it was to gain funds for college. The truth of the matter is I am not sure why I made that decision beyond liking my recruiter and seeing a glimpse of who I wanted to be in him. I always knew I would go to college but I did not know how to get there. I knew my mom did not have the money nor the pathway plotted for me to go, but if I was ever going to become the great architect I longed to become, I would have to go to college at some point. The Air Force was something to do. After all, my mom had told all of us all of our lives that when we turn 18, we have to "get out of the house." She told us, "you going to School, work, Army, getting married or something, but you getting out of here." When asked about that declaration now, she denies its validity, but all three of her children were gone from home before age 18. Think it not strange.

As the bus pulled out of the recruitment office parking lot, I waved good-bye to my mom and Sergeant Tom McCray. I shed tears of uncertainty, as I was unaware of what was to come of me or for me. I had enlisted for four years. The made a trek down Highway 31, across Highway 20, and eventually stopped at the Huntsville Recruitment Office. There, several individuals boarded the bus and we rode in relative silence to Nashville, Tennessee, where we would formally enlist at the Military Entrance Processing Station (MEPS).

Along the route from Decatur to Huntsville, I read the note my mom had given me. As I read it my tears flowed in streams of uncertainty about the future and certainty of an unrelenting love between a mother and a son. We had a very close-knit bond that had been tested greatly at that point, but it did not break under pressure. I left home knowing I was loved and she let me go knowing when all else failed our love would succeed.

After the bus filled in Huntsville, I chose to put the note away out of fear I would cry in front of the other recruits. Now I wonder what they were holding back. Had they left home frantic, anxious or afraid? Was this an escape to or from something? I did not ask and I do not have answers from them but I learned through my four year experience that each enlisted came to Lackland Air Force Base for many different reasons. Those same recruits departed Lackland, after basic training, holding to those same reasons and aspirations or they did as I did and let the needs of the military dictate movement and progress, while making the best of every situation.

I did not know what to expect when we got off that bus in Nashville. I had not even thought about how we would get from the MEPS in Nashville, Tennessee, to Lackland AFB in San Antonio, Texas. A recent graduate of Auburn University, Kevin Waldrop, was also going to Lackland that day. Since he was a college graduate, he was placed in charge of me and another young man. Kevin was responsible for leading us from the Nashville airport through DFW Airport and on to the Air Force Reception Area at the San Antonio Airport. This was the first time I had ever been on an airplane. Whew!

So, of course as they for young men boarded the tram at DFW, 24-years after I had made a similar journey, my thoughts went back to that first flight and all that has transpired since. I had no idea what shape or path my life would take. I had no way of knowing how challenging or rewarding my military experience would be. No one could prepare me for the growth I would undergo in six short weeks - growth that continues today as I trace it back to that bus ride from Decatur to Nashville, and the plane ride from Nashville to San Antonio. But I know the experience was enriched as I went through that experience with Kevin. We did rely on each other for spiritual and moral support.
All of us need others to make it through difficult and unfamiliar stretches of our journey. I had my mom's love, Kevin's presence and my tattered Bible as I made my transition from civilian to airman. All were necessary and all were maximized to ensure my sanity and success.

Those four young men were full of energy and vigor...and my prayerful support remain with them as they grow and serve together.

As those young men and all other military service personnel give of themselves for others, may their experiences in life and love be rewarding and life transforming. As they encounter people from many villages, cities, tribes and nations, may they be calm and confident in knowing their strength and purpose.

May they truly discover the best of who they are on and off the battlefield? May they solidify bonds with people who eat different types of food and speak various languages? May they see the world as a smaller, interconnected place than they may have been led to believe? May they explore questions of faith and order in the world - no–withstanding fortifying their hearts to follow orders and directions that churn at their core?

May they always have support of family, common soldiers, and friends - now and forever? Amen.

Thoughts On An Awkward Moment

November 2011, two men were exchanging greetings. It appeared they knew each other from a past life or at least were socially familiar with each other until one of them asked: "How's your father?" The response, "He died in '94!"

The next 17 seconds were filled with as much silence, anxiety and as much wanting for attention and interaction as the previous 17 years. That was a pregnant pause in need of a Lamaze class and an epidural. It was equally as painful for the onlookers as it was for those, well-educated, distinguished gentlemen who now stood on the brink of a breakup or a breakthrough in their relationship. What were the right next words to utter, or was silence the virtue of choice that would usher them and us into a new reality?

Silence, when it comes as a result of an awkward encounter can accost the mind, body and soul, causing involuntary reflection that can lead to wisdom based responses or fear-facing tactics that satisfy our need to retreat or to repent. It was obvious those men had not seen each other for quite some time or if they had, they had not conversed about anything as meaningful or as relevant as the health and well-being of each other's loved ones. It was that or the one man confused the other with some other casual acquaintance. Regardless of how the men and all of us ear-hustlers ended up in the space, we were now forced to reckon with how we would handle the same situation, whether we were the one posing the question or the one offering the blunt and honest response.

When we are faced with moments that push us into corners, we ensure the old theory of fight or flight holds true. We fight back with excuses or misgivings about what someone failed to tell us or include us in prior to that moment. We find fault in systems and relationships that could have created the blockage or barrier. We fight our ego's battle to be better and find a way for it to save face as it experiences ultimate exposure or humiliation. When we do not fight, we evade and avoid the situation - pretending the words were not spoken or the person did not mean what they said. Clearly we are not being understood or we are being taken for granted or being taken advantage of. At any rate, we say "we are separating ourselves from this 'mess' and will find solace in another venue or relationship that will not hold us back as this one has. When in fact, what is viewed as 'being held back' may in fact is 'being held accountable.'

In the end, we are responsible for maintaining good communication in relationships with those near and far. We are responsible for caring for watching over one another and speaking the truth to one another in love. We are responsible for holding each other in those awkward moments - not deserting each other because of our inabilities to cope. If one cannot bear the burden or call the other to task, then what is the value of the relationship? Whether it's a 17-minute conversation or one that spans beyond 17 years, mutual respect love and support will sustain a relationship.

Even when time has passed and little has been spoken between friends or casual acquaintances, the desire to stay engaged when you do not know how sets one in a vulnerable position but it also sets both in position to be honored, cherished and loved into the future. It lessens the ego bruising or swelling that comes when we ask questions or deliver information that will bring sudden silence and awkwardness to the fore of the mind, relationship and to the door of any room full of familiar strangers.

Great, and merciful God, forgive me when I speak too much and when I speak too little. Grant me a spirit of discernment that comes from being in conversation and fellowship with you. Grant me wisdom that comes from your heart and your Word. Grant me patience while I wait, listen, and learn. May I speak with tongues of angels and express love in every situation – even when my knowing is not as it should be. Amen.

Thoughts On Room of 1000 Demons

Psychologist, Author, and Speaker, Dr. Barry Hart (*see References*), shares a story centered in the Tibetan monk tradition where every five years the monastery opens the Room of 1000 Demons as part of their training.

All of the candidates are brought to the exterior of the room and it is explained to them that inside the room there are 1000 demons and each them are aware of the candidate's worse fears. He writes, "For example, if you hate spiders, once in the room you'll find yourself among 1000 of the worst kind of spiders imaginable." Of course many candidates opt out of the experience and very few remain open to facing the challenge. Prior to entering the Room, the candidates are told to remember 2 things: 1) "None of the demons are real;" and 2) "Keep moving your feet."

It seems a simple lesson and one that I know intuitively or on some minimal level. However, I have often found myself facing fears and anxieties that lack a source in reality. The reality upon which they are based is someone else's reality. This is not to minimize physical danger or even psychological trauma inflicted upon me at some point. Those things happened and they were real. But, I am no longer in that same place.

I have other experiences and other relationships to factor into the equation. I have the option to stay where I am and continue experiencing the pain, fear and anxiety that has held me back or I can choose to keep moving – determining not to stay in a place where fear reigns supreme. I can choose to face my fears and eventually leave them behind. I can also choose to allow my past to dictate my future, while it diminishes my presence and impact in the world.

Lord, have mercy. Give me strength to face my fears and to keep moving toward you. Amen.

Thoughts On Church and Politics

I stand amazed when I hear people say, "The church is too political." But, those are the same people who use the Bible, their biblical understandings and theological underpinnings to influence legislation and elected officials to stay within the bounds of what has been deemed holy or right.

When there are at least two sides to every issue, one God and one majority, how does a system, its laws or its participants move to a place where marginal and minority opinions and voices are considered? The question is not about biblical literacy, as all can read the same texts and come away with vastly different understandings. The question is not about theological prowess, as there are publications and scholars for every camp. The question is not about agreeing or disagreeing, as there is clearly a divide along those lines. So then, what is at the core of the argument(s)? Is it about winning and losing or whining and listening?

In my work as a conflict mediator, I am keenly aware that folks often begin by shoring up their evidence to support their opinion, which bolsters their arguments in favor of their position and interests. But, where we find the most usefulness is when individuals and group can be honest about their needs. When needs can be clearly stated, there is a depth of understanding that can be reached because most people can recognize need. It is in sharing needs that closer, if not common, ground can be realized. However, that destination is but a blip on the screen when people are committed to leaving the room or the argument with exactly what they brought into the situation. It takes conversation.

Sometimes in politically charged processes conversation takes on the feel and flow of protest and civil disobedience. At other times active defiance is the way to get people to the Table or to force a vote in favor or in opposition.

During the 2012 General Conference sessions, I overheard several people saying: “Why do we have to always talk about homosexuality? It always divides people and we leave in pain over those votes. Why can’t we just not talk about it and see how things go?”

Well, those folks are the same ones who believe the church is too political and must be about spiritual matters. On one level I totally agree – we must be about disciple-making conversations and actions. But, what is missed by those folks is that some of those would-be disciples are not welcomed into our churches and are in danger of losing their livelihood because the church will not have conversations that allow for an acknowledgment of a variety of biblical and theological interpretations.

The church is not as big as God is. The world is bigger than the church, but the world is not as big as God is. The Word is big and covers many practical and historical matters, but the Word is not as big as God is. An even more poignant fact is that the Word informs us that God is love. That leads me to believe that love is the only thing we can conceive or express that can even begin to compare to God and God’s vastness. God is big enough to love every realm of possibility and expression in the world and in the church.

Our politics and theology are constructed for those inside to keep those outside the church outside the church. That may not be the stated intent, but it is a consequence of our actions and inactions. That holds true on a variety of realities faced by folks who rely on the church to inform them of moral imperatives and daily choices that impact their existence. But, who listens to the voices beyond the wall? The purpose of the wall is actualized when we gather to protest opinions and propositions. The height of the wall is magnified when we shout for holiness inside but do not respond to the cries for justice on the margins.

It does not matter if the issue is Divestment, Guaranteed appointment, Apportionments, Episcopal authority, Abortion, Adoption, Same-sex marriage, or Lay Speaking ministries, there are needs, interests, and opinions that must be shared and shaped from within the church and from beyond the church. We must engage in real conversation because what we deem holy conferencing is anything but *holy*.

Regardless of what I want, I must pause, think, and pray about it. I must consider that what I believe may be based on some truth or precept that some deem antiquated while others revel in its relevance. I must be willing to acknowledge that the church has a political strand within its DNA and I cannot ignore it, no more than I can be afraid of it. The church once ruled the world, so politics is at its core, but that does not have to be a liability each time we engage one another.

When Christians cannot agree that they disagree, the question rises to the level of questioning what it truly means to be Christian within the context. It is clear there is disagreement within the church, not just one denomination, on several issues but who will be the first to say: "Our core issue is not about theology, but it is about hospitality?" Who will rise to that level and challenge the church to be a place of hospitality? Hospitality demands love and care be extended beyond all else. How about we start by extending hospitality to our neighbors? How about we follow that by extending hospitality to the familiar strangers in our sphere of influence? How about we follow that by extending hospitality to our family members who have made choices we would not have made? How about we follow that by sitting with one person with differing opinions and interests and asking what are their needs?

Shall we begin with politics or hospitality?

Lord, have mercy on us.

Thoughts On My Last Tear

Whenever I approach an intersection, freeway exit off-ramp, or the entrance to a store and there is a woman or man asking for financial help, I wonder how they ended up in that place. What decisions did they make or fail to make that created this situation? Then I realize I am no more than 1 paycheck and 2 decisions away from that same predicament.

Lord, I want to cry my last tear today. I am so sick and so tired of not knowing what to do. I just keep crying about how things are in the world. Then I cry about how things are not in the world.

When I think about the wars and the seemingly senseless killing that takes place around the world to fulfill ill-sought-after power or wealth, I cry. When I think about the children who spend their nights sleeping on the streets or sleeping in beds where men, and women alike, take advantage of them, I cry. When I see mother's struggling to feed and clothe their children by means that pull her and the children farther into the gutter, I cry. When I see fathers finding importance in street credibility, I cry. When I see young girls fighting to be women and women fighting over a man, like young girls, I cry.

Lord, I want to cry my last tear today. For that to happen I think you need to show up in all these situations that I see on a daily basis. I want to cry my last tear today. Is that possible? I believe you can do all things. Is it possible? I suppose the problem here is that I will continue to cry until I truly realize that I can do all things through Christ who gives me strength to be present and active – working for liberation on behalf of all those who are oppressed and neglected.

Lord, I want to cry my last tear today, but knowing what I know...I need the strength that only you can give to allow me to continue this journey, with tears.

Thoughts on Strength

My mom used to always say, "Lord, give me strength!" I wondered why she asked that question. Why did she need the Lord to give her strength and what would she do with it when she received it? Now that I have lived a little while longer, I know why she prayed that prayer. I know why she called on the Lord to do what only the Lord could do.

Lord, give me strength.
Give me strength to bring all my burdens and misgivings to you. Give me strength to hold on to the truths of your word until my change comes.

Give me strength to let go of the things that keep me from growing closer to you. Give me strength to let go of the things that keep me from growing closer to others. Give me strength to stretch my spiritual ear and to open my heart.

I want and need all of these things so that I can become better acquainted with your voice. I want and need all of these things so that I can better acclimate to the direction you have charted for my life.

Lord, give me strength to make it through this day and to experience at least one more victory.

Keep whispering to me, if that's how you are speaking to me. Keep shouting at me, if that's how you are speaking to me. Keep providing significant relationships in my life, if that's how you are speaking to me.

Keep me asking 'Am I doing to the right thing?' if that's how you are speaking to me. Keep speaking to me until I hear you clearly and follow you exactly as you command.

Lord, I know you can give me strength. Amen.

Thoughts On Healing

Two long-time friends accompanied each other to a local clinic for their bi-annual HIV test. One of the young men was always afraid of a positive diagnosis, while the other felt his presence there was more for moral support than for the test. Well, this particular trip yielded information that neither was prepared to hear. The one who was always terrified left the clinic with his normal *negative* diagnosis. The other left holding a piece of paper and several pamphlets that confirmed his *positive* status.

God, you said in your word that when we are sick, we should call on the elders and they will anoint with oil, pray the prayer of faith and the sick will recover. You said in your word that by your stripes we are healed. You said in your word that you withhold no good thing from those who walk upright.

You may have noticed that I know what your word says. I know that there are promises of wholeness and healing in your Word. The problem here is that I have figured out how to get the words off the page and into my head, but I have not gotten the word from my head into my heart. I do alright assuring others of their success, salvation, healing and deliverance, but I fail miserably at affirming my own faith of a brighter today and hope for tomorrow.

I want desperately to believe that you will heal. I want desperately to believe that you will touch his body, his heart, his mind, and his soul and you will take the pain and the doubt away.

I want to be able to lay my head on the pillow and know within my heart that you have me in the palm of your hands. That's what I want. I need to let you hold me and to trust that what I perceive as inactivity, could be your way of waiting for me to be still and know that you are God. Heal all who are wounded, scared, broken, sick, abandoned and ashamed. And so it is!

PRAYERS

Jesus taught the disciples many things they would need to continue the ministry and transformative work Jesus launched in their midst, but he did not leave them to their own devices when it came to prayer. When they asked about prayer, he gave them a prayer to pray. That tells me that Jesus knew the importance of prayer in the life of a disciple.

Prayer is an essential part of any faith journey. Development of faithful practices are built upon various prayer forms. Any spiritual discipline introduced to an individual or community is rooted in prayer, whether it is internal and introspective or external and expressive, it begins with an acknowledgment of who God is and an expectation of God's presence and participation.

Prayer is as important as it is a creative enterprise that everyone can do in any place at any time and it cannot be done incorrectly. The prayers on preceding pages and on the following pages are samples and examples of the many names of God and a sampling of the many facets of our lives that must be considered in prayer. Pray on, prayer!

A Prayer For The Real Me

Lord, you know my every weakness and you know how comfortable I am hanging on to my shortcomings.
You know I am scared of letting go and allowing you to take control of my life, particularly the areas that I try to hide from you and from others.

What would people think if they knew the real me? What would church folk think if they knew all there is to know about me?
What would my siblings think if they knew I sometimes struggle to do the right thing? What would my friends think if they knew I sometimes choose to do the wrong thing, in advance? What would my neighbors think if they knew I love you, but I sometimes struggle with how you show your love?

Would their knowledge of my weaknesses make them stronger? Would their knowledge of my true character cause them to be any less of a Christian? Would it demonstrate that all of us, regardless of our calling, struggle to find our place and struggle to let you show your strength in and through our weaknesses?

Sometimes I just don't understand the point of all this. At other times I see exactly what you are trying to move me toward. I am grateful for those times and I am grateful for those glimpses because they give me the strength I need to do what I need to do for you and in your name – in spite of my failing love and my excuses for not following you faithfully, every step of the way.
You know I would if I could, but right now I do not have the faith and fortitude it takes to let you have it. I ask that you continue to work with me and my issues.

Prepare me with strength and courage to trust you, to hear you and to respond to your call for total surrender. Thank you for calling out to me, and for calling me your own, even when you know I pretend I do not hear you. Amen.

A Prayer In This Moment

Let us give thanks.

In this moment, we are grateful for this day and this opportunity to be together. In this moment, we are grateful for what we have received and for what we have given.
In this moment, we are grateful for those we hold near and dear to our hearts, and for those we have only known by way of fleeting encounters. In this moment we are grateful for times when we were fully present, and for times when we were conveniently absent.

In this moment, we are grateful for what we have accomplished on our own, and for what only succeeded because we were part of a team. In this moment we are grateful for this season, when we are mindful that the gifts discovered in familiar strangers are just as valuable as those among us – the wounded healers.

In this moment we are grateful to be here, to be servants, to be aware of this moment.
To have the choice of what we will or will not eat.
To have the choice to sit where we wish.
To have the unconscious choice, but certain knowledge, of where we will sleep tonight and tomorrow night – safe and warm.

In this moment, we are grateful for those individuals and circumstances that cause us to pause, to be grateful for what has been, for what is, and for is to come.

So, this day, this prayer is much simpler than our much-too-complicated lives.

For this (occasion, food, honor, etc.) and for this fellowship, we are grateful. Amen.

A Prayer To End Each Day

God, you made me and you know me.

You are the one who decided that I needed to become a part of your world. Although I love you and appreciate all that you do to keep me in this world, I sometimes wonder "why" and "how" am I to find and to fulfill the purpose you set for me.

I try to focus my thoughts toward you but sometimes I stray from what I believe you want me to do, to say and/or to be. I desperately desire to be complete in you. I long for my life to be transformed from what it is to what you destined. So, I ask you God, to begin to reveal to me, in ways that I can understand and comprehend, what you want me to do, to say and to be. I ask you, God, to continue to be patient with me, as you increase my patience for others and for me.

I really want to get this right. I really want to pray as a Christian ought to pray. I really want to believe in you as a Christian ought to believe. I really want to testify of your goodness as a Christian ought to testify. I really want to get my life in order.

I would also like for those closest to me to gain an understanding of who you are and what you have purposed for them, also. I do not wish to be selfish. I want the best for all those whom I know and love. Transform my heart and mind so I might testify and win them and their hearts for you.

I ask these things of you, my God, because I believe you will answer me. I do realize that your answers are not always instant, nor are they always what I desire. However, if Job trusted you through his ordeal, then surely I can trust you through mine. Thank you for taking this time to listen to me.

I love and adore you. Amen.

REFERENCES

Translations of the Bible

CEB Common English Bible. © 2010, by the Christian Resources Development Corporation in the United States of America. All rights reserved.

NIV New International Version. © 1978, by Zondervan in the United States of America. All rights reserved.

NRSV New Revised Standard Version. Scripture quotations, unless otherwise noted, are from the *New Revised Standard Version*, copyright © 1989, by the Division of Christian Education of the National Council of the Churches of Christ in the United States of America. All rights reserved.

OTHER MATERIALS AND NOTATIONS

"In This Moment" was a prayer written along with a dear friend who had something specific he wanted to convey in a public setting. What is published is a compilation of his sentiment and spirit and my words. The prayer may be adapted for use in a variety of settings.

"House of 1000 Demons" may be accessed at the following: http://ezinearticles.com/?expert=Barry_Hart

DISCLAIMERS

Names of individuals and companies have been changed as much as possible, so as not to draw attention away from the crux of the story and to avoid instances of liable, slander or breaches of confidence.

ABOUT THE AUTHOR

I am a work in progress. I look around and see people and things that make me think in different ways. I am seeking new and creative ways to connect with God and my neighbors.

If you would like to chat about any of the Thoughts and Prayers contained in the book, or if you wish to extend an invitation for me to be present with your congregation or group, please contact me:

Cedrick D. Bridgeforth
P.O. Box 561765
Los Angeles, CA 90056

pastorcedrick@gmail.com

www.thoughtson.org

www.cedrickbridgeforth.com

www.ingramcontent.com/pod-product-compliance
Lightning Source LLC
Chambersburg PA
CBHW060514030426
42337CB00015B/1885
9780978694418